INTEGRATED COST AND SCHEDULE CONTROL IN PROJECT MANAGEMENT

INTEGRATED COST AND SCHEDULE CONTROL IN PROJECT MANAGEMENT

Ursula Kuehn, PMP

𝔪

MANAGEMENTCONCEPTS

MANAGEMENTCONCEPTS

8230 Leesburg Pike, Suite 800
Vienna, VA 22182
(703) 790-9595
Fax: (703) 790-1371
www.managementconcepts.com

Printed in the United States of America

Library of Congress Cataloging-in-Publication Data

Kuehn, Ursula, 1949–
    Integrated cost and schedule control in project management/
    Ursula Kuehn.
        p. cm.
    ISBN 1-56726-170-1 (pbk.)
    1. Engineering economy. 2. Project management. 3. Cost control.
    4. Scheduling (Management) I. Title.

TA177.4.K864 2006
658.4'04—dc22   2005054362

ABOUT THE AUTHOR

Ursula Kuehn, PMP, is president of UQN and Associates, Inc. She has been a certified Project Management Professional since 1995 and a consultant/trainer to government agencies and commercial corporations in various aspects of project management. She has a strong background in operations research and mathematics, and she specializes in integrated cost and schedule control and earned value management system procedures. Her educational accomplishments have earned her an MS in operations research from the George Washington University (GWU), a Masters Certificate in project management from GWU, and a BS in mathematics from Bowling Green University. She is a member of American Mensa. When she is not working, she and Fred can be found sailing their 41' ketch, the *S/V Julie Marie*. She can be contacted via email at ursula@uqnandassociates.com.

TABLE OF CONTENTS

Figures

Exercises and Solutions

PREFACE

When we were children, or even later when we went to college or started our first jobs, I doubt that many of us said "...when I grow up, I want to be a project manager." I certainly didn't. I wanted to be a ballerina, maybe you wanted to be a fireman. But, thanks in part to a sister who wanted to be a teacher and who taught me to add, subtract, multiply, and divide before I entered elementary school, I excelled in mathematics. After my secondary education I earned a BS in mathematics and lasted one year as a math teacher in an experimental middle school.

After a short stint as a bartender, I landed a job with a consulting firm working with Goddard Space Flight Center doing quality testing of satellite imagery. During this time I decided to go back to school to pursue a higher degree and was convinced by a counselor, because of my math background, to choose operations research. I eventually earned an MS and proceeded to use my newfound knowledge in pursuit of a career performing reliability studies and statistical analyses.

Most project management techniques stem from the field of operations research. Operations research includes the study of business analysis, network analysis, decision analysis, and simulation, all of which provide the basis for many of the tools and techniques used in project management. Once I acquired the degree, it would seem preordained that I would be doing what I am now doing in the arena of project management. But it didn't start out that way. I started experiencing many of the notions I will be presenting long before I obtained that degree. I just had not "connected the dots" yet.

With another consulting firm working with Goddard Space Flight Center, I was assigned to a project to determine the attitude specifications of an orbiting satellite. When my project manager asked me how long it would take to do my part, I told him three days. He obviously didn't believe me because he gave me a month to complete the task, which fit into his delivery schedule, rather than using my talents to get other tasks accomplished. I was taking university courses at night to obtain my masters degree, so I took advantage of the time by studying and doing homework at work for three weeks. I started the assigned task at the beginning of the last week and finished it a day early. The customer loved what I produced, but my performance appraisal disparaged me for "lack of initiative." This was my first encounter with "bad" project management.

Shortly after completing my degree I was employed by a consulting firm contracting with the Department of Defense. After doing a fairly good job on my first assignment analyzing the reliability of some Army communication headsets, I was asked to come into my manager's office and heard those words that many of us have heard: "You're doing such a good job that we are going to make you a Project (Manager) Engineer ...." This firm had yet to embrace the term "project management" because that seemed like a "soft skill." (I was also told on a number of occasions that mathematics was a soft skill.) Nonetheless, the notion of "You the PE" instilled a feeling of accountability that far exceeded any I've experienced since.

I must admit I took on this assignment with some trepidation, as I had no idea what I was doing on the management side. The technical (and social) side of the project, which was to have an Air Force Security Police vehicle tested at a secure site in the Nevada desert (about an hour from Lake Tahoe) for six months was right up my alley (skiing and sailing are my two favorite hobbies). I was told that our company had an in-house course that would teach me all I needed to know to manage the project. This course taught me how to plan the tests and schedule my effort for each test, as well as how to chart my actual expenditures against my planned expenditures. I was to return to headquarters each month for a project review.

During my first project review, my actual expenditures were lower than planned and I was told I was doing a great job. This continued to be true for my second, third, and fourth project reviews, during which time my customer was asking for new tests to be performed. "What the customer wants, the customer gets." It was at the time of the fifth project review that the actual expenditure line crossed over, that is, went above the planned line on my graph. This was when I realized that there was more to this management process then just tracking planned versus actual expenditures. I wasn't taught how to track what was really being accomplished for the expenditures and how to determine how much money would be needed to complete the project. I had to "bite the bullet" because my project was going to come in over budget.

After this episode, I lost the title of project engineer and was eventually assigned as a project team member on a project managed by someone who finally showed me what management and leadership were all about. He had a way of making the team "want" to work for him by allowing everyone to participate in the planning and ultimate success of the project, but what I thank him most for is when he figuratively "slapped me across the face" by saying, "Ursula, you have a degree in operations research. You should know this stuff." I began to grab as much reading material as I could find to quickly learn what this process was all about.

It wasn't the reading that caused the "eureka" moments, though. Many of the books I read had a lot of interesting and enlightening words in them, but none seemed to tell me just how to do it. I remember waking up in the middle of the night saying, "I get it. It's so simple," after reading a huge book on how to use earned value analysis to control the cost and schedule of projects but which never told me how to calculate the earned value. I soon realized that I was going to learn more about the subject of project management by experience and intuitive reasoning. My experiences and reasoning served me well because I took the Project Management Institute's certification test for a Project Management Professional (PMP) in 1995, without taking any classes in project management, and passed it on the first try.

It was in 1993 that the most enlightening moment about controlling cost and schedule occurred. I had acquired a fondness for sailing and had become an accomplished team member on a racing sailboat. I found myself complaining quite a bit about having such a hard time finding good sailing gear to fit me. I remember complaining the most about my inability to find a decent pair of sailing gloves to fit my small hands. I was told by a clerk in a marine supply store that "women don't need good sailing gloves because they don't do any of the hard work on the boat." I saw the need for something, or someone, to show the manufacturing world that there were a lot of women not only sailing, but also racing sailboats. To help fulfill that need, I undertook a project to start a small retail company, produce a catalog for women who sail, and supply whatever products I could find that women could use on a sailboat.

I put together a business plan and was approved for a small business loan to undertake this endeavor. I hired a graphic artist to produce my catalog and this is where the true essence of the project management process began to unfold. My graphic artist asked me what kind of catalog I wanted. I looked at her in amusement and replied " … a catalog-catalog, like I get in my mail every day." Luckily this graphic artist knew more about integrated cost and schedule control then she probably realized herself because she broke "a catalog" down into all of the major parts of producing a catalog: paper, color, copy, photographs, graphics, printing, postage, etc. She showed me estimated costs for each of these parts and forced me to take a look at my small business loan budget and see what I could afford.

After a bit of negotiation we settled on a six-page, black and white brochure with a splash of teal, with photos that I would take myself and mailing preparation that I would convince my friends to help me with. It wasn't until we had gone through this process that together we could begin to plan this part of the project to get the catalog out on time (I had secured a booth at the U.S. Sailboat Show) and within my budget.

After my experience with the catalog, the pieces all fit together. Controlling the cost and schedule of a project is an integrated process of balancing the scope to the budget to the time. Over the years many tools and techniques have been developed to help us control this integrated process. In this book I describe this integrated process and share some of the many tools and techniques that I have learned and used on the many successful projects that I have been lucky enough to help manage.

We all manage projects every day. Most of us have just never taken the time to learn the process and to see how this process will make our daily lives more efficient and fun.

I've written this book to reach the reader who has never been introduced to the integrated process of cost and schedule control but is willing to learn. I also have geared the book to the more experienced project manager who would like to learn something new or something he or she has never thought of in this manner before. I use simple examples, most of which are projects around my house, to demonstrate how the tools and techniques work.

In Part 1, Chapter 1 presents some basic concepts of project management that that are the underpinnings of many of the concepts discussed throughout the book. Chapter 2 addresses just what is meant by integrated cost and schedule control. I define the integrated process as a number of overlapping sub-processes and show how the results of these processes help guide the project to a successful result.

In Part 2, Chapters 3 through 5 take the reader through the steps of performing the initiation process, one of the subprocesses defined in Chapter 2, where the project deliverable is defined. The emphasis of these chapters is on defining the scope of the "best deliverable that the customer's budget can afford." This is the most important step for controlling the cost of the project.

In Part 3, Chapters 6 through 10 take the reader through all the steps of the planning process, another subprocess defined in Chapter 2. The emphasis in these chapters is on building and analyzing the schedule of the work identified in the initiation process introduced in Part 2.

In Part 4, Chapters 11 through 13 take the reader through some essential steps of the execution process and the controlling process, also defined in Chapter 2. The emphasis in these chapters is on baselining the plan, gathering information about the progress of the work being executed, using earned value techniques to determine the status of the cost and schedule aspects of the project, insulating issues that affect the cost and schedule, and resolving those issues.

Last, Part 5 presents some techniques for closing the project properly.

So, before we start into the actual process, I present a number of basic concepts that I believe lay the foundation for an overall understanding of the nontechnical aspects of integrated cost and schedule control. The subsequent chapters then show how the puzzle pieces work individually and how they logically fit together to work toward the success of managing a project.

Ursula Kuehn
Annapolis, Maryland

ACKNOWLEDGMENTS

Writing a book was something I always told people I would never do. My excuse was that I was an instructor and I wouldn't know how to put my arm flailing and other gestures on paper. I'm not quite sure who it was that caused my brain to stop listening to all my excuses.

First and foremost, I thank my students, who brought to my attention that they couldn't find many books that taught them "how to do it." They would say that there were plenty of books that told them what project management is, but very few that actually taught them anything they could actually use. They wanted a book that they could refer to that would help them recall how the process works and how the tools and techniques can be used in their jobs and their daily lives. Here you go. I'm taking you through all those examples we talked about in class.

I would like to give a huge acknowledgment to my good friend Toni Hodges DeTuncq, who authored *Linking Learning and Performance* and shared with me all the tools and techniques she used in writing her book.

I also thank Arnold Hill and Tim McConaghy, who both gave me the opportunity to try my techniques on their daunting projects and to prove to myself and to them that those techniques really did work. I want to give special thanks to Tim for helping me edit this book while he studied for his Project Management Professional (PMP) certification exam.

Above all I thank my friend and love, Fred Miller, who put up with my confidence swings and took quite a bit of his own free time to help copyedit this book. I also thank him for his encouragement throughout this process.

PART 1

PROJECT MANAGEMENT AND THE INTEGRATED PROCESS

1 BASIC CONCEPTS

Before exploring the various tools and techniques of integrated cost and schedule control, a number of basic concepts must be understood: What is success? What makes work a project? What does project management mean? Who are the people involved in the project? How important is documentation to the project?

SUCCESS

To understand how integrated cost and schedule control techniques work, we first have to understand the psychological aspects of "success." We all have mortgages, rent, and/or car payments to make, which means that we all have to get up each day and go to work to earn the money to make these payments. One of the best feelings in the world is getting ready to go to work knowing that you'll be spending your day working on something that will be successful. This is such a good feeling that it puts a spring in your step. You have a tendency to get more done because you want to keep the good feeling going. We all can think back on how it felt to work on a successful project.

The flip side is that one of the worst feelings in the world is waking up and getting ready to go to work knowing you'll be spending your day on something you know will not work, or will not get done on time, or will cost too much, or no one will really want or use, or with which the customer will be unhappy. This is not a good feeling. Not only is there no spring in your step, but you're probably taking longer to get ready for work than normal. You have the tendency to get less done because you don't really care. We all can think back on a project we worked on that had no chance of being successful and how that felt.

A basic understanding of what makes work successful is the most important part of what integrated cost and schedule control is all about. Whether you are the only one working on your project or you have a team helping you, understanding success even if it is the delusion of success is what enables the work to get done. We all need a sense of accomplishment.

Success is the goal that is tantamount to everything we do to control the cost and schedule of the project. That means we must define the project and everything we think might happen on the project as clearly and realistically as possible. We must make sure that we describe the work unambiguously and that the work is attainable. We must use all available tools and techniques to control the project to the best of our abilities. This does not mean that we cannot make the work challenging, but it is self-defeating to expect something to be accomplished that simply cannot be accomplished.

THE PROJECT

Another basic understanding required for integrated cost and schedule control is an internalization of two basic definitions: What is a project? and What is project management? A lot has been written about these two basic concepts, yet misunderstandings abound.

Project Management Institutes' (PMI®) *Guide to the Project Management Body of Knowledge (PMBOK®)*[1] defines a project as

---

[1]*A Guide to the Project Management Body of Knowledge, Third Edition (PMBOK® Guide)* (Newtown Square, PA: Project Management, Inc.), 2004.

"a temporary endeavor undertaken to create a unique product or service." The *PMBOK*® readily points out that organizational work generally falls into one of two categories, operational work and project work, and that projects are undertaken at all levels of the organization.

Tom Peters, in his book *In Pursuit of Wow,*[2] defines all work as project work in the new economy. He says that work should always add value, and that if it adds value, it is a new, unique endeavor.

Many organizations seem to think that larger projects should no longer be known as projects, but should be called "programs" instead. This view often stems from the notion that we have to promote project managers to the higher position of "program manager." If the work has a beginning and an end and creates something new and unique, it is a project—no matter how big or small. A program, on the other hand, is usually made up of a collection of projects, but goes beyond the completion of the individual deliverables, through the operation and support of the deliverables, to what is often called the "end of service life" of the deliverables. Understanding that cost and schedule control techniques can be applied consistently to very large, complex projects as well as to small weekend "house" projects will go far in making the work proceed more easily and efficiently.

PROJECT MANAGEMENT

Project management is not a title, nor is it a job description. In fact, it is a process that should be learned and understood by every level of the organization. It is amazing how many people call themselves "project managers" but have very little understanding of the process. Worse yet are the many upper-level managers who believe they are "above" learning the process. These upper-level managers do not seem to grasp that the bet-

---

[2]Tom Peters, *In Pursuit of Wow* (New York: Vintage Books), 1994.

ter all the members of their organization, including themselves, understand the project management process, the higher their chances for overall success within their organization. Instead many of these upper-level managers impede the opportunity for success by not supporting the project management process.

Everyone can do and does projects. Aside from what we do at work, we all have projects underway at home, in our neighborhoods, and at our clubs or places of worship. Planning and managing these projects enable us to get them done. How many times have you set out to accomplish that Saturday morning project, just to find yourself running back to the hardware store in the afternoon? If you had used good project management processes, that might not have happened.

STAKEHOLDERS

Anyone who can "help" or "hurt" your project should be viewed as a stakeholder. Your customer, the users, your management, your team, vendors and suppliers, or other departments that you will depend on, can all "hurt" your project if their needs are not considered. For example:

- The customer who is never happy with the outcome and constantly wants more

- The user who doesn't use the deliverable of your project

- Your manager who doesn't provide the support your project needs or who micromanages your project because he or she doesn't trust your abilities

- Other internal functional managers who refuse to support your project or to give your project the priority it deserves

- Your team members who do not buy in to the project

- Support organizations, such as Purchasing or Finance, that refuse to support the requirements of your project

- Vendors, contractors, and suppliers who do not meet their agreements and do not deliver.

Each stakeholder has specific needs that must be determined, considered, and possibly included in the scope of the project. Getting the stakeholders involved and enthusiastic about the project is crucial to the success of cost and schedule control.

THE PROJECT TEAM

The project team is a subset of stakeholders who can either do major damage to your project or be your most valuable asset. The project manager's leadership abilities will determine which way this goes. The project manager needs to understand and appreciate that unless he or she can do all the work of the project, a project team will be involved.

Some of the best project managers realize that the less autonomous decision making they do during the initial and planning stages of the project, the more leadership stature they maintain throughout the project, because no one can accuse them of making that "bad" planning decision. They encourage involvement of all the team members, which in turn encourages "buy-in" to the project objectives and ultimately to a focus on the cost and schedule control of the project.

The composition of the project team can change substantially throughout the project. For example, the initial project team may be a group of subject matter experts who have the customer familiarity and technical knowledge to assist in defining the overall deliverable. This composition of the team should change based on whether a different potential team member has the skills or knowledge to take over the definition or decomposition of the deliverable from a certain point in the project. The composition of the project team could go through many iterations until the entire scope down to the true definition of the work involved to complete the scope is defined, at which time the resource that can best do the work should be identified and should become a member of the project team.

THE PROJECT MANAGER

The project manager is you: you, who has been asked to get something done and to have it done by 2:00 p.m., or by Friday, or by the end of the month; or you, who recognizes a need and believes that you can take care of that need in time to make a difference; or you, who has taken on responsibility for delivering that unique (be it ever so slightly unique) product or service.

It doesn't matter how big or how small, if the product or service is needed, is something unique, and is required to be delivered by a certain time, it falls into that definition of a project. The words "I need it by ... " is what makes it a project. The first step of taking on the responsibility of being a project manager is to make sure that whoever is asking for "it" realizes that "it" is never free. Producing anything takes time and time is money; the management challenge is to make sure the requester can afford "it" and that the time is efficiently planned to get "it" done.

Another aspect of project management is that "it" may be needed to accomplish a different project. In other words, the project that you are managing may be a subproject of the project that whoever requested "it" is trying to manage. This makes your "customer" another project manager.

The realization that all projects are interrelated allows for overall efficiencies of good project management. All workers should recognize the project aspects of their work and how the tools and techniques of integrated cost and schedule control can help them in accomplishing that work.

In today's world we tend not to recognize an individual worker as a "project manager" until he or she has taken on the responsibility of a large, complex project. The assigned project manager who has not considered him- or herself a project manager before must quickly learn project management tools and techniques. This can be a daunting task, especially when the individual is "thrown to the wolves" well into the lifecycle of a project.

Too often the inexperienced project manager thinks he or she must be "the expert" and should take on the role of defining and planning the entire project. The enlightened project manager knows that this is not true. Some of the best project managers have no technical expertise in the deliverable of the project. They know that their responsibility falls more in facilitating a group of experts (i.e., a project team) to define what the customer deliverable should look like. The project manager doesn't need this expertise, because the project manager usually is not the person doing the work; however, the project manager must know how to use the terminology of the technical aspects of the deliverable. In other words, the project manager does not need to "walk the walk," but he or she had better know how to "talk the talk" if they are to maintain their credibility with the project team and stakeholders.

The process of allowing other team members to participate in identifying and decomposing the deliverable, along with the realization that all projects are made up of many subprojects, enables the project manager of a large, complex project to delegate portions of that project to various team members and to assign them as project managers of their subparts.

PROJECT DOCUMENTATION

Good project managers embrace documentation. They understand that documenting everything they do, every process they intend to use, and every decision or assumption they make keeps everything having to do with the project on a business level as opposed to a personal level. Aside from being a mechanism for better communication with all the stakeholders involved in the project, documentation is CYA—"cover your activities" or "cover your assumptions."

The project charter is one of the first and most important documents of the entire project management process. The *PMBOK®* defines a project charter as "a document provided by the project initiator or sponsor that formally authorizes the existence of a project, and provides the project manager with the authority to apply organizational resources to project activities."

The project charter provides so much more than that. It provides the history, or the "why" the project is being undertaken in the first place. More importantly, the project charter provides the "outer boundaries" of the project by providing the budget constraint (i.e., how much the customer can afford) and the time constraint (i.e., when the customer needs the deliverable). If you truly believe, as I do, that every project is a subproject of someone else's project, there would be a number of project charters that "pass down" or delegate authority for the parts of the deliverable of your project to each of the team members who are expected to deliver their parts.

The idea of identifying every team member as a project manager of their subproject, providing them with a project charter that defines their boundaries, and teaching them each the project management process gives those team members "ownership" of providing a deliverable to the customer (which might be you.) The team member/subproject manager quickly learns that they need to perform a requirements analysis and define the "best solution" to meet those requirements.

2 THE INTEGRATED PROCESS

"Time is money," to quote Benjamin Franklin, and that is no more true than when trying to control the cost and schedule of a project. This is why it is so essential to understand the processes, techniques, and tools of defining a project based on the cost of the time it will take to produce the overall deliverable of the project.

In this chapter we will introduce the integrated project processes, the balancing technique crucial for cost and schedule control, the binding structure tool that will be used throughout the integrated processes for cost and schedule control, and the idea of having a baseline and steering the cost and schedule of the project within a predefined tolerance threshold.

THE INTEGRATED COST AND SCHEDULE CONTROL PROCESSES

As defined in the *PMBOK®*, the process of project management entails five subprocesses. These individual processes are called many different names by different organizations, but it is the understanding of what happens during each that is important. Using PMI®'s terminology, the subprocesses are the initiating process, the planning process, the executing process, the controlling process, and the closing process:

- The *initiating process* is where decisions are made about whether something truly will take care of the need and can be afforded in light of the customer's budget. This decision authorizes the "parts" of the deliverable or service of the project, which in turn define what is in the scope of the project and what is not. This is where the customer's or stakeholder's expectations of what they will receive are balanced, based on the money they have in their budget. Setting these expectations allows control over the project's cost and schedule. We will explore this process in depth in Part 2, because it is the most important and most misunderstood process in project management.

- The *planning process* is where the best method of accomplishing the work in time for the customer to use the deliverable (identified during the initiating process as the agreed-to scope) is explored. Too often this process gets started without the initiating process having been performed, and project plans that are not balanced go forward into execution. These imbalanced plans have little or no chance of success. Carrying out the planning process effectively requires a basic understanding of network analysis and statistical analysis. These techniques are presented in a straightforward fashion in Part 3.

- The *executing process* is where the work gets done. This process relies less on management techniques and more on leadership abilities. Some of the management techniques that are involved in the other processes, such as including the team in the initiating and planning processes and guiding the project toward a successful completion, put the project manager in a "leadership" position with the project team.

- The *controlling process* establishes a guidance system for the performance of the work, in terms of both time and cost, and redirects the planned work, where required, to stay within the control area of that system to a successful completion. This is where earned value analysis is so useful; we address how this analysis is performed in Part 4.

- The *closing process* puts accomplishments "on the shelf" and analyzes them for lessons learned and their usefulness in the future. We address these techniques in Part 5.

Many unenlightened project managers see these sub-processes as distinct and separate phases. They envision the entire project plan as one big waterfall schedule through the lifecycle of the project, as shown in Figure 2-1.

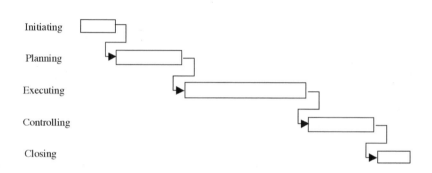

Figure 2-1. Project Subprocesses Planned in a Waterfall Schedule

This type of schedule often becomes "very expensive wall-paper," because the schedule doesn't realistically show how the subprocesses are performed in real life. In the real performance of any project, the subprocesses tend to overlap through the lifecycle of the project, as shown in Figure 2-2.

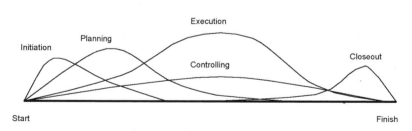

Figure 2-2. How the Subprocesses Overlap during the Project Lifecycle

Understanding how information passes from one process to another allows the project to be planned in an iterative process that more closely emulates real life. Another way of saying this is that to get to the point where we have truly defined the work of the project, we need to have done a lot of the work of the project.

BALANCING THE TRIPLE CONSTRAINT

The key to being able to control the cost and schedule is having a plan that balances the scope of the deliverable of the project with the customer's budget and has the right resources assigned at the right time to perform all the work in time for the customer to be able to use the deliverable. This is called the triple constraint (see Figure 2-3).

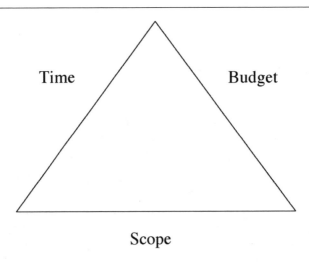

Figure 2-3. The Triple Constraint

This triple constraint must be balanced during the initiation and planning processes if the cost and schedule of the project are to be controlled through the execution and closeout processes.

It is a delicate balance because some of the time and money are expended just to get to the point where the initiation and planning are complete. To maintain this balance throughout the project, the project manager must always be aware of where the project is in each process.

To maintain this balance, terms such as "quality" or "resources" come into play. The idea of quality has to do with defining the scope that fits the customer's budget and will be able to accomplish what the customer plans to do with the deliverable. For example, the customer may want a Cadillac but not be able to afford one. The need that is being addressed is the fact that the customer needs transportation and a car is a "class" of deliverable that can fulfill that need. The quality (attributes) of the deliverable (scope) has to be balanced with the customer's budget. If the customer demands the quality of a Cadillac, then the need to have transportation cannot be met until the budget for the Cadillac is available.

Resources take time to get work done. Two resources can usually get a job done faster than one if they have the proper skills and the scope of the work has been unambiguously defined. If there are not enough resources to get all the scope of the deliverable completed in time for the customer to use it, one option is to reduce the size or the quality of the scope to something that the resources can complete and the customer can still use.

As the project plan is time-scaled, the costs involved to complete the work can increase as a result of factors such as escalation. This is why incremental planning, with budgets defined for each increment, is used on many projects. Incrementally funding the project based on defined releases of the deliverable has mitigated some of the risk involved in balancing the triple constraint of large, multiyear projects.

This is all one big balancing act. Those projects that are not balanced are virtually impossible to control no matter how much earned value analysis is done.

THE WORK BREAKDOWN STRUCTURE

The one binding tool through the entire integrated process of cost and schedule control is the deliverable-oriented work breakdown structure (WBS). The deliverable-oriented WBS is a tool used in every process. It is built during the initiating process by recording the decomposition of the deliverable and helping determine the work items required to build the deliverable that will take time and effort to accomplish.

The effort of these work items translates into money that will help balance the scope of the work to the customer's budget. Like with my She Sails catalog mentioned in the Preface, my expectations, like any customer's, were not set until I was presented with how much each part cost and I realized that I could not afford everything I originally wanted.

The time required to complete each work item, which is identified using the WBS for the agreed-upon scope, will then become part of the schedule. That schedule will then be used to plan how each of these work items will need to be accomplished for all of them to be done in time during the planning process.

Because these work items are "children" of the parts of the scope, the WBS/schedule shows the progress of the project during the execution process. The WBS also presents the information for performing the analysis that will help us control the work items during the controlling process. This approach of using earned value information presented in the WBS will also help us isolate issues while they are small and can be resolved during the controlling process.

It is important to understand that a deliverable-oriented WBS is a tool for integrated cost and schedule control. Too often project managers use other methods of developing a WBS, such as a time-oriented or task-oriented structure.

The time-oriented WBS has the tendency to set up the first level of the WBS based on "milestones." For example:

1.0 Project

    1.1 Requirements Analysis

    1.2 Design

        1.2.1 Preliminary Design

        1.2.2 Detailed Design

    1.3 Implementation (or Build or Code and Unit Test)

    1.4 Test

Each major part of this time-oriented WBS is an ambiguous term that can neither show the customer what they are going to get at the end of the project nor help the project team figure out the work that will need to be planned for the project. In most cases, when this method is used, the only opportunity to see that the triple constraint is not balanced comes toward the end of the project when the only recourse is to eliminate testing.

It is true that a good practice, especially when a project is very large and will expend a lot of budget, is to break a project down into phases of time. Each of these phases, however, must be identified as a subproject and a deliverable that needs to be produced. The WBS needs to focus on that deliverable and all the subdeliverables that make up that deliverable to be produced for that phase.

Keeping in mind the first, basic understanding of success, work to define the project and everything you think might happen on the project as clearly and realistically as possible.

U.S. Department of Transportation
Headquarters Relocation Project

Back in 2001 I was asked by a student to look over a WBS for a new building planned for the rehabilitation of Southeast Washington, D.C. The manager of this project showed me something that reminded me of the many schedules I've seen in the past that were filled with ambiguous terms and claimed to be work breakdown structures. He told me he had paid a consultant quite a bit of money to help put it together (what I like to call "very expensive wallpaper").

He happened to have a small whiteboard hanging on the wall of his office, which I used. "Arnold, you're building a building," I said and proceeded to put a box at the top of the board that said "Building." "If there is just one building, then you break that down into subground, walls, floors, etc. If there is more than one building, you break it down into west wing, east wing, guard shack, and then proceed to break each down as though it is a separate subproject."

I sat through many sessions with the project team creating the WBS. It was interesting when the contractor in charge of installing all the IT hardware presented a WBS that was based on the typical milestones with ambiguous terms (e.g., preliminary design). We refused to accept it and had the contractor redo it based on the breakdown of the building. They claimed to have never constructed a WBS in that way, but agreed that it (1) made sense and (2) would be far easier to estimate the costs.

When I explained to all the team members how this deliverable-oriented WBS would serve as a better management tool during the actual construction of the building, I had them all converted. If the budget for 2007 gets cut in half, for example, then the building WBS can be prioritized to identify a possibly usable portion of the building (say the east wing) that can be completed for the 2007 budget. The rest can be rescheduled, with all the tasks that are associated with completing the rest of the building, to the following years.

It takes time and effort to develop a project work breakdown structure. The requirements have to be known before you can complete the WBS, but the WBS serves as a tool that records the decisions of the requirements analysis and focuses the analysis to smaller and smaller components of the project. The customer should see exactly what they are going to get in the WBS.

To this day, Arnold still carries that white board around with him.

THE GUIDANCE SYSTEM

Using the integrated cost and schedule control tools and techniques during the subprocesses of initiating and planning the project results in a project plan that ultimately is locked in as a baseline. This baseline then serves as the guidance system of the project because it points to the goal of getting the agreed-upon scope completed within the customer's budget and in time for the customer to use it.

This project baseline is similar to a flight plan that the pilot of any airplane must submit before the flight. The pilot charts a course that points to the destination of the flight. If you ask a pilot how often he or she is exactly on the flight plan, they will likely tell you that they are on the plan at take-off and at landing; in between, they might happen to fly through it. Yet, they all seem to be able to fly to their destination with very few problems.

If the plane is not exactly on the flight plan, the pilot can usually steer the plane back. If not, the charts are brought out to develop a new flight plan. Hovering close to the flight plan is what allows the plane to reach its destination.

In project management, it's not being exactly on the baseline of the plan that counts—it's that you can steer the project team back toward the baseline. Using the tools and techniques of integrated cost and schedule control allows the project team to identify "control areas" around the baseline (like flight control lanes for a pilot) both on the positive side and on the negative side that the project status should stay in to be successful.

If a pilot finds him- or herself outside the control lane, with no possibility to steer the plane back in, the pilot would need to contact someone to make them aware of the situation and to be directed out of the way of other traffic, determine a new flight plan and submit it for approval, check the fuel to see if they will need more than what they have (budget), and report to the passengers, "We'll try to make up as much time as we can."

Projects go through the same process. If the project status is outside the threshold of the control area and, no matter what the project team tries to do, the status is doomed to stay outside the control threshold, the baseline of the project is no longer serving as a guidance system. The project should be replanned and the baseline should be changed via a change control process. Someone needs to be made aware of the situation (through a change request) and the impact to the scope, budget, and/or schedule must be determined. If approved, more budget or resources should be added to the project or the due date of the project should be adjusted, all of which will change the baseline so that it serves as a truer guidance system for the rest of the project.

Now that we have a basic idea of the process, the triple constraint, the WBS, and the guidance system, let's see how these processes of integrated cost and schedule control really work.

PART 2   THE INITIATION PROCESS

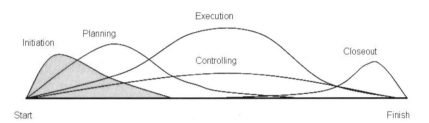

The initiation process is the most important process involved in controlling the cost and schedule of the project. This process defines the "what" of the project through the delicate balance of two sides of our triple constraint, the scope and the budget. The initiation process focuses on whether or not we should do the project or any part of the project, based on the needs and wants of the customer and how much money they have. In other words, the scope of the project is defined during the initiation process.

The initiation process involves three basic steps:

1. Defining the scope and identifying the work packages required to build the deliverable

2. Estimating the effort, cost, and duration of completing the identified work packages

3. Balancing the scope to the customer's expectations and budget.

3 DEFINING THE SCOPE

To define the scope of the project's deliverable, decisions must be made about whether or not a deliverable or service will meet the customer's need and still fit into their budget. These decisions should be based on the answers to such questions as:

- Does the customer need it?

- Does the customer want it?

- Will it benefit the customer to have it?

- Can the customer afford it?

- Do other stakeholders need or want it?

- Will it benefit other stakeholders?

- Will it enable the project to be executed more efficiently?

The answers to these and other fundamental questions allow the project manager to truly focus this decision-making process regarding "what" is in the scope of the project on true objectives. Finding these answers takes time and a lot of work. The initiation process cannot be considered complete until the entire scope of what is to be built on the project has been designed or at least defined and agreed to by the stakeholders.

CUSTOMER-FOCUSED SCOPE DECISIONS

All projects stem from a customer need. The basic steps that start the initiating process are:

- Identifying the customer, stakeholders, and users

- Determining the difference between a need and a want

- Controlling the ever-changing need

- Clarifying the misunderstood need

- Differentiating among the needs of multiple stakeholders or users.

Although the initiation process is the most important, it is the most misunderstood of the five processes of project management. The initiating process usually involves a lot of time and a lot of work. In many cases, it could take the entire allotted time of the project, because many of these decisions are held off until the end to "see how much money is left over." Too often this up-front work is never accomplished, which can have detrimental impacts on the project during the execution process.

Consider building a house. We all need shelter, and there comes a time in almost everyone's life that we either want to buy a house that is built from scratch or an existing house that needs improvement. If we have already talked to the bank, we have an idea of just how much our budget is and what initiating types of decisions need to be made. If we don't go through a good process, we run the risk of never being satisfied with the outcome of the house.

Let's consider some bad decision scenarios:

Bad decision scenario #1—Not building a case for the need for a house in the first place.

How many people do you know who just went out and bought a house, any house, the bigger the better, to later find that they could not keep up with the payments, ended up with more house than they could ever use, or just weren't happy with the house they bought.

Making a good case for why you want the house, what the house will provide you in the future, and whether or not you can afford the house and taking the time to find the right house to fit these needs is essential to your overall satisfaction. No one wants to be stuck with a house that is too big or too small, that you don't like, or that you can't afford.

Buying a house is a project, just like any other project. Before we enter any project, a case for the project should be developed (sometimes referred to as a "business case"), defining exactly why the project is required, how the deliverable of the project will be used, and what we think we might receive in return for taking the time, effort, and budget that we will expend to obtain that deliverable. This business case helps focus the project team on not trying to build more than what is needed by whoever will use it.

Bad scenario #2—Not realizing that, even though we have found the right size of the house we want, we may not be able to afford it.

Just because you decide to buy a small, one bedroom, one bath house on an inexpensive lot does not in and of itself mean that you will be able to afford it. Whether or not the house is affordable depends on all the little parts that go into the house.

How many times have you opened that magazine or catalog and seen those perfect marble floors that would look so good in your kitchen? You want those marble floors right up to a certain point. That point, of course, is the moment you see just how much those marble floors cost.

Just like with the house, all projects have budgets. Making sure we provide the best solution that the customer can afford is tantamount to the overall success of the project.

CUSTOMER EXPECTATIONS OF WHAT THEY CAN GET FOR THEIR MONEY

The goal of the initiating process is to make the decisions about what will go into the deliverable and present to the customer exactly what they are going to get for their money. The best technique for accomplishing this is to conduct various reviews of the scope, using the WBS, with the customer so that the customer gets a chance to see what the deliverable will look like and how much the parts of the deliverable are likely to cost. This in turn allows the customer to have a say about whether they like or want the deliverable or any part of the deliverable, whether they would rather not have it for this iteration or release, or whether they would rather not have it at all. Although it may be difficult, we need to hear the customer say that they "do not want that." This enables the customer and the project team to reach agreement on the scope of the project.

In most cases the customer is not exactly sure what they want, yet they expect the project team to be able design exactly what they want. Customers have been known to declare, "I'll know it when I see it." If the project team doesn't take the time to go through the initiation process and never allows the customer to "see it" on paper before they build it, "it" could end up not being exactly what the customer expected at all. The customer will then start expressing their wants and preferences as the deliverable of the project is being built in the execution subprocess.

This is what causes those "creeping requirements" that so many projects experience. A detailed description of exactly what the customer is going to receive and how much it is going to cost is never presented, agreed upon, and baselined; thus, the customer thinks they can get anything they want.

Creeping requirements, also known as "creeping elegance," have produced more project failure than any other issue of project management. If the customer hasn't agreed on what type of floor should be installed and the installation of a linoleum floor has already started, the customer could change their mind and complain that they expected a marble floor. Then the cost of installing the linoleum up to this point must be added to the cost of de-installing the linoleum, the cost of designing the new floor, the cost of installing a new subfloor that can handle the weight of the marble, the cost of acquiring the marble, the cost of the installing the marble, and the cost of supervising and inspecting the job. This new cost of the kitchen floor will be much higher than the original estimate, causing a cost overrun on this part of the project that should have been avoided in the first place.

As I mentioned in the Preface, it was after this experience with the She Sails catalog that the pieces of the project management process began to fit together for me. I realized the importance of the initiation process and how the decomposition of the scope of the deliverable was the most important of the subprocesses. We broke the catalog into parts, estimated the cost of each part, and were then able to make the decision of "what" should (or could, dictated by my budget) go into my little project. This step of scope decomposition and cost estimation, and the subsequent analysis of what my catalog really did require, gave the project a chance of being successful. Had we not done that, my "customer expectations" would have remained way too high and my relationship with the graphic artist would have deteriorated, which ultimately would have led to the demise of the project.

BUILDING AND USING A DELIVERABLE-ORIENTED WBS

The most important tool of the initiating process is the deliverable-oriented work breakdown structure (WBS) (introduced in Chapter 2). The purpose of project is to deliver a specific, unique product or service; the decomposition of the scope is what forms the deliverable-oriented WBS into an architectural breakdown of that product or service.

The central focus of a deliverable-oriented WBS is the overall deliverable of the project. For example, if you are constructing a building, then the top block of the WBS would be the building. If you are developing software, then the top block would be the major function the software will perform for the customer. My favorite example is building a pond in my yard, where my top block would be "Ursula's pond." I would have to develop a business case of sorts to justify why I need a pond. I certainly would have to manage the pond. I know I'll have to design the pond and test the pond, but the rest of my subdeliverables are going to be the major parts of the pond.

To start my decomposition, I would need to perform a requirements analysis. This is a process in itself where the project as a whole and each part of the project are scrutinized to make sure that they meet the need of the customer or stakeholder and, also, that the part fits into the budget. This analysis is like "peeling an onion." Through the analysis, the parts of the scope are identified. Then through a structured tool of documenting this decomposition of the scope (the WBS), the requirements analysis can be focused down the structure to each individual part.

Let's see how the WBS can help me plan my pond. Let's say that I would like to complete the entire pond in a weekend. If I were to use a task-oriented WBS, as described in Chapter 2, breaking down the project into the tasks of design the pond, build the pond, and test the pond, I can almost guarantee that I will not be able to complete the project in a weekend. It is very difficult to identify all the work that is, anything that might take time on the project using this type of WBS. If I don't identify all the work that might take time, I will not be able to plan for it in my schedule and by the time it becomes obvious to me that that additional work will need to be done, it will be too late.

By doing a requirements analysis, I can identify the major parts of the pond, such as a hole in which to place the pond, a liner, and water. Note that if a requirement for this project was to not break the ground surface, then the basic major parts of the WBS might be a plastic tub and water. The output of what is determined by my requirements analysis is the input to my deliverable breakdown, which in turn allows me to decide what goes into the scope of the project and what does not.

For this example, let's say that the basic requirements of my pond are a hole, a liner, and water, plus some livestock and some attractive plants. Our structure might look like the top-level structure shown in Figure 3-1.

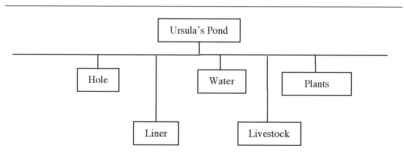

Figure 3-1. High-Level Breakdown of Ursula's Pond

There could have been several more major parts to my pond, like a stone border, a water treatment, or external landscaping. There also could be many logistical deliverables that relate to the pond as a whole, such as training (possibly broken down into operation and maintenance), equipment needed to maintain the pond, user documentation, supplies, etc. These initiation subprocess decisions are made based on the requirements and the budget. They then should be documented (remember CYA) in the business case.

The requirements analysis can now be focused on each of the individual major parts of the project. Let's take "hole" as an example. What is required to have a hole? The basic two functions that need to take place are to remove earth from the ground and to dispose of the earth. We could look at each of these functions as a subproject in itself: "earth removal" and "earth disposal."

Performing a requirements analysis on the subproject "earth removal" might include a requirement to study the geological drawings of the area where the earth is to be removed. This study would further define whether a backhoe or just shovels will be needed, or maybe even dynamite depending on the matter to be removed. In other words, this study is part of the requirements analysis but might never have been identified as work that would take time if we had not analyzed this part of the WBS. This geological study may also identify other required deliverables, like an environmental study.

A study to locate any utility lines, as well as many other time-consuming activities, might need to be performed before any earth is removed from the ground. But that is the whole point of the WBS—it is the tool that helps identify anything that might take time in the project, and since that time usually translates into money, it helps determine if we really can afford to do the project within our budget.

"Earth disposal" might be another subproject. For example, the initiation process decision may be to use the earth taken out of the ground to build a garden in another part of the yard. This subproject would require its own breakdown of major parts.

Let's take a look, in Figure 3-2, at what the WBS of the hole might look like.

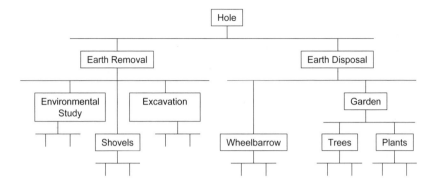

Figure 3-2. WBS of Hole

Notice that the lines under subdeliverable "hole" and the two subprojects extend further than what we've identified. That's because work packages—in this example, those actions that need to be undertaken to remove the earth or dispose of the earth—have yet to be added to our WBS. Work packages are the lowest level of any branch of the WBS where resources will be assigned responsibility. Let's take a look at what types of actions or work packages can be identified so far in our structure.

The pond, as a whole, will need to be designed. This design of the pond will probably be a drawing of what the entire pond should look like once it is completed. The drawing should show each of the major parts of the pond that we decide will be part of the scope through the initiation process. Keep in mind that this work package can be broken down further into individual tasks, such as conducting a site survey, developing a drawing, and having the drawing reviewed and approved by the customer. You could almost say that this is a project in itself (which goes along with Tom Peters' philosophy that all work is project work, mentioned in Chapter 1).

The pond will need to be tested. Maybe this will involve nothing more than an inspection that will take too small an amount of time to track on the project, but it will take time nonetheless.

In other projects, a test might be further broken down into such work packages as developing a test plan, identifying various test scenarios, performing the tests, writing the test reports, etc., each of which could be broken down even further.

Now let's take a look at the hole for the pond. The hole will need it own design. This design is different from the pond design because the hole needs a drawing that shows how long it should be, how wide it should be, how deep it should be, and where the shelves to hold those plants that need water but do not like being at the bottom of the pond (e.g., "bog plants" needed for filtration) should be constructed. A test will have to be conducted to make sure the hole will hold the plants properly. This test will take time and that time needs to be included in the project plan, especially if you want the project completed over a limited period of time, like a weekend.

The method for removing the earth has to be determined. An environmental assessment may need to be performed before any earth is removed. Do we need to buy a shovel, rent a backhoe, acquire some dynamite? If we build a garden with the removed earth, then the garden will need to be designed, and so on.

Now let's look at the subdeliverable "water." Three major functions have to take place to have water in the pond (which are very similar to any project that must deliver an information system, often referred to as an information technology, or IT, project): (1) water has to get into the pond (input of information), (2) water has to circulate (processing and storage of information), and (3) at times water has to be drained from the pond (distribution of information), as displayed in Figure 3-3.

Each of these functions can be deemed a subproject. For example, "water in" could mean an entire plumbing system that pumps water from a water source to the pond. Often a landscape artist who specializes in ponds will contract this out to

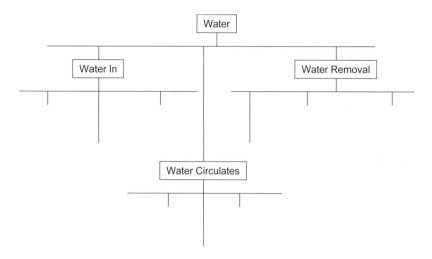

Figure 3-3. Breakdown of Water Subdeliverable

someone who specializes in plumbing systems. The details of this plumbing system should be broken down by someone who is familiar with all the requirements of this kind of system.

Water circulating would require a pump, which in turn requires electricity, which might be another subproject where a certified electrician might be needed to run a new electrical line from the power source of the house to the area of the pond for the pump to plug or tap into. A water treatment or waterfall that might be one of the major components of the pond would need to interface with this pump via a hose or tubing that would have to be purchased. This water treatment may require a more powerful pump. Filters for the pump will be required. In other words, the circulation of water is a project in itself.

Water draining might also require an environmental study, depending on how and where the water is to be drained. An actual drain might need to be buried, which would change the requirements of the subproject for earth removal.

Again, the work of each of these identified subprojects and components takes effort that will cost money and will take time. Accordingly, decisions about whether or not to include these subprojects and components in the scope of the project need to be made before any of this work can be planned. I'm not sure who first said it, but you can't plan what you don't know. The WBS, here in the initiation process, is the tool that helps us figure it all out or at least as much of it as we can.

To many in the software product development world, a deliverable-oriented WBS is still quite foreign. This world still wants to base its WBS on time phases, not the functionality of the software. They have yet to understand that the WBS should be based on the functionality that the software is supposed to deliver to the customer, not time. If the WBS is broken down in the same manner as the architectural breakdown of the functionality, then all the different designs that need to occur at each level of the functional breakdown would be defined as individual work packages and, depending on the number of resources that have the skills to do the individual designs, the work can be scheduled over time in a much more efficient, overlapped manner.

FSTAI Software Company

One of my very first consulting jobs was to help a small software development firm. The project manager complained to me that the project was behind in the "code and unit test phase." I told him that the only way I would be able to help him would be to take the team off-site and facilitate the redevelopment of their WBS. He agreed to bring me on to give it a try.

I brought the team to a conference room and proceeded to ask them about "what" their software would do for the customer. Each time they told me the functionality, I wrote it on a Post-it® note. I would then go to each functional part and continue to decompose it based on "what" it would do for the customer. At the end of this exercise, I had the full functional architecture of their software on the wall on Post-it® notes.

I then put a design Post-it® note and a test Post-it® note on each function and put separate design, code, and unit test Post-it® note on each function point at the bottom of the structure. I explained to them that this is what the WBS should have looked like. They, of course, told me that they had never done a WBS in this way.

I then took the design of the whole software Post-it® note and asked if that work package was completed. They all chorused "yes," so I threw it away. I proceeded down the structure to each sub-function's design Post-it® note and asked the same question. The higher-level Post-it® notes were all thrown away, but when I got to a fourth-level design Post-it,® the project manager said "yes," but the team stayed quiet. After some time, a team member volunteered that this was one of their problems that the design of that function-ality had yet to be completed. I then put the Post-it® note back on the wall, at which time the project manager said, "but I have a design document approved and signed off." It was obvious that the dozen or so people expected to review and approve the design document had no real idea what they were reviewing.

The flip side of this was that a number of function points had completed their design, code, and unit test. When I asked why these function points were not being integrated and tested as higher-level functionality, I was told, "We can't. We're not in our test phase yet." So there was a lot of design work that had not started yet and a lot of test work that was being artificially held off because of their "phased" approach.

Worse yet was the feeling the team members had been getting that the project was a "failure." Once their success with the inte-gration and testing at the various higher levels of functionality was recognized, the team was able to develop a recovery plan and within two months they had the project back on track.

To have a complete set of work packages for the deliverable-oriented WBS, each subdeliverable, or component part, of the overall deliverable will require its own design work package and its own test work package, plus any logistics that are specifically focused on that subdeliverable (e.g., training, equipment, manuals). Each of these subdeliverables could be deemed sub-projects, which means that they each will need work packages addressing their specific design, test, logistics, etc. It's the part in the middle (the "build") that usually involves one of six decisions:

1. Are we (the project team, under the leadership of the project manager) going to build it? If so, we probably should continue to break it down.

2. Have we already built it (a part on our shelf, or a reusable software function previously coded) and can we get it "off the shelf"?

3. Is another department in our organization or company, over which we have no control, going to build it? If so, should they be asked to break it down further?

4. Have they already built it and can we get it from "off their shelf"?

5. Do we need to have an outside vendor build it, which will require a contract that should ask them to break it down further?

6. Has an outside vendor already built it and can it be acquired from "off their shelf"?

Often I've seen the expression "Buy COTS" (commercial off the shelf) used in a project plan as one task. I often wonder how anyone estimates how long that takes or how much that might cost. I'm often told that the procurement department is responsible for defining what it is, how long it will take, and at what cost. But "buy COTS" is a very ambiguous term that is meaningless to anyone until each item to be bought is specifically defined. The project managers who include this in their project plans are not delegating, but are instead abdicating responsibility for this part of the initiation process. Admittedly, the initiation process is hard to carry out, but abdicating responsibility and using ambiguous expressions for work does not make it easier.

Once we have defined the scope of what the customer needs and wants, we need to develop cost estimates for each of the parts of this scope so that the customer's expectations can be balanced to their budget for the project.

4 ESTIMATING THE COST AND DURATION OF WORK PACKAGES

Nothing is free. The customer who gets work accomplished for free will see it as just that—nothing. They will constantly want more because they assume it doesn't amount to anything. Even if we give our customers a deliverable for free, we need to make sure that they understand the value of what they just got and that somebody paid for it.

Various techniques are available for determining the cost and duration of the effort that will be needed to develop the scope.

DETERMINING WORK PACKAGES

The work package is the lowest level of any branch of the WBS and is that point where the further breakdown of the component or part can be assigned to a member of the project team. That team member could work directly for the project manager, work in another department of the organization, or be a third-party vendor. In all cases, the person assigned to the work package should break the work down further. Doing so makes work packages SMART:

- *Specific*. If the team member (whether a direct report, someone working for another department, or a third-party vendor) cannot break the work package down, then that package is not specific enough for the team member to know what he or she is expected to do. The project manager must provide more information to the team member until they are able to visualize the deliverable part that they are being assigned responsibility for and are able to decompose it. Without this, the team member will not perceive success in accomplishing the work involved in providing the deliverable part of the work package.

- *Measurable*. If the work package is broken down further, it can now be measured based on the breakdown.

- *Attainable* (or agreed to). The team member and the project manager can agree that the breakdown fully defines exactly what the team member is expected to do, which will help avoid surprises during the execution process of the project.

- *Real* (or realistic). The work package produces a deliverable part, which is real.

- *Time-oriented* (or time-constrained). By allowing the team member to break the work down, his or her estimate of the time it will take to complete the work will be more realistic. The project manager may then be able to compress that time by providing resources that can help complete the work package more quickly.

Another outcome of asking each team member assigned to a work package to make it SMART is that the team member is now gaining knowledge about the initiation process of project management. This learning helps develop the team member as a more useful resource for the organization in the future.

ESTIMATING WORK PACKAGE EFFORT

Once the work packages have been identified using the WBS, the work is estimated. This estimation of effort, along with any materials, equipment, etc., translates into a cost estimate for the work package, which can be used to perform a bottoms-up roll-up of estimated costs to balance the scope with any predefined budget. The goal is to identify the best solution that the customer's money can buy. This balancing must take place or the project will be doomed to fail before any work has started.

How do we estimate work? There is a tendency to estimate work based on the question "How fast can I do that?" After we've determined how fast we think we can do the work package, we then "pad" it because we know things can go wrong. In many cases there is then a tendency to double our estimate because we suspect (based on past experience) that someone "up the line" will cut it in half. (Of course they cut it in half because they suspect that we doubled it ....)

The problem here is: If I think I can do a work package in three days, add two days to allow for things going wrong, double that to 10 days, and then my manager accepts my estimate and enters 10 days in the plan for my work package, my manager has just given me permission to take 10 days to complete a work package even when nothing goes wrong.

Knowing that I fall into that "student category" described by Eliyahu Goldratt in his book *The Critical Chain*,[3] I will put the work off until three days before the 10th day, when it is due. This forces me to be able to get the work package done in 10 days only under perfect circumstances. If anything goes wrong, it will probably take longer than 10 days.

We all tend to estimate in this manner, especially when we build our project estimates based on only one estimate of each work package. By using just a single estimate, we're setting ourselves up for failure from the start (see Chapter 8 for a detailed discussion). But before we even discuss the notion of getting more than one estimate for each work package, let's examine the concept of estimating. Without estimating cost, we cannot complete the initiation process of project management.

---

[3]Eliyahu Goldratt, *The Critical Chain* (Great Barrington, MA: North River Press), 1997.

To estimate the cost of a work package, we first have to estimate the effort it will take to complete the work package. Then we can determine the cost of materials and other expenses that will also be needed to complete the work package and that, with the cost of labor, will translate into an estimated cost for the work package.

The three basic methods of estimating the effort that might be needed to complete a work package are:

- *Pure guess*—which, like it or not, many times we must use

- *Analogy*—making our estimate based on a similar work package that was performed in the past

- *Parametric*—basing our estimate on a number of similar data points of performing similar work packages in the past.

The pure guess is a method that no one would use if they had better information, but when the project deliverable is something that is brand new, innovative, etc., using a pure guess of the effort to complete a work package is inevitable. In most cases, however, taking the time to break the work package down further provides portions of almost any "brand new" or "innovative" work that are known and have been accomplished previously, which in turn isolates the unknown part to something that may encourage a more realistic guess.

If a work package from another project that is similar to the one we've identified in the WBS of our current project can be identified, then an analogy can be made to the previous work package's actual effort information collected via timesheets. This information, once it is adjusted appropriately for any uniqueness, can be used to develop our estimate of the effort required for our newly defined work package.

If the actual effort for a number of work packages similar to our newly defined work package was collected, then a parametric of the average amount of the actual effort of these work packages can be used to estimate each similar work package. Another method of using parametric estimating to estimate effort is possible if we have been able to produce productivity factors, such as meters of pipe installed per hour in construction or lines of software language code developed per hour, from past similar project components or work packages. For example, if I can determine, from past similar project work packages, that on average we have a productivity factor of 2.8 lines of software code per hour, and if I can estimate that our newly identified software function point work package will require 300 lines of code, then my effort estimate for this work package is approximately 107 hours of effort.

The best tool for capturing actual information in a manner that is useful for future estimating of work package effort is the deliverable-oriented WBS, in which each work package is a child of a lower-level component, part, or function that builds up to the components and modules of the deliverable of the project. This type of WBS produces information that is repeatable and can be correlated and traced, when needed, to a similar component part or functional module of the work package currently being estimated. The information also can be stored in a central repository with information not only from your organization but also from other organizations that can be used to support the estimating process.

The construction industry has been able to accomplish this. Reams of parametric data are available on-line to assist in the estimating processes for constructing a building. The software industry has been slower in accepting the deliverable-oriented WBS that produces the repeatability required to produce this parametric information. The Software Engineering Institute (SEI) is on the right track with its Capability Maturity Model (CMM®), which expects organizations that produce software products to develop repeatable processes for capturing information.

Many of the software- or IT-producing communities with which I have worked still have no better method for estimating because they collect their information from past projects by phases or time blocks that are defined in ambiguous terms, such as preliminary design, detailed design, code and unit test, and integration test. Actual information about the design phase of one project cannot be correlated with actual information about the design phase of another project because the deliverables being designed are usually very different.

What often surprises me is that they do take the time to design an architectural breakdown structure of the software or the system, but they don't seem to make the connection that this structure defines their deliverables and should also be used in developing their WBS. The structure defines to the customer what they plan to build so why shouldn't this same structure have all the work added to it? The resulting deliverable-oriented WBS will be far more manageable.

INCLUDING RISK IDENTIFICATION IN WORK PACKAGE ESTIMATES

Murphy and his sister Miss Hap seem to be involved in every project. We have all seen these two characters in our past projects so we can usually figure out how they might look in our current project. We call this identifying risk.

A risk is an identifiable future event that has a probability of happening and will have an impact if it does happen. Risks can be identified only from past events and because we have a tendency to remember adverse past events more than those that worked in our favor, we tend to think of risks in the negative (i.e., threats) as opposed to the positive (i.e., opportunities). Either case can be used in developing an estimate of the effort of a work package; however, when things go well they tend to shave off only a slight amount of effort from the work package. When things go wrong they tend to add quite a bit of effort to our work packages. It is for this reason that "padding" an estimate is the norm, and is done with the best of intentions; however, as previously shown, it does not always lead to the intended outcome.

A better method of incorporating risk identification into our estimating process is by first asking for four pieces of estimated information for each work package: (1) a most likely estimate for completing the work package, (2) an estimate for completing it if everything goes perfectly, (3) two or three things that could go wrong while completing the work package, and (4) how long would it take to complete the work package if all of them happen.

Let's use as an example: changing an oil filter in a car. When I ask a volunteer in my class who has experience changing the oil in his or her car how long it takes to just change the oil filter, they usually quickly respond "10 minutes." I remind them about having that perfect wrench that fits on the filter and loosens it quickly, the filter coming off and the gasket coming off cleanly with it, that box saying it's the right filter for your car and it turning out to actually be the right filter when you open the box and it having a gasket, putting a little oil on the gasket, threading it on "hand-tight," and adding just a little quarter twist. I then ask them, under those circumstances, how long would it take to change the oil filter? It's amusing how many of them look at me strangely and say, "Well, ah, 10 minutes," which proves my point that most of us think, "How fast can I do it?" when first estimating. I then let them use 15 minutes as their most likely estimate.

I then ask them, "What can go wrong while changing an oil filter?" Everyone in the class usually wants to chime in at this point, because if we have any experience with this at all, we've all experienced the Murphys and the Miss Haps of changing an oil filter. They will call out such things as: the filter is stuck (it's amazing how many students all over the world have tried the old screwdriver-through-the-oil-filter trick); the gasket didn't come loose, the phone rings; the oil spills on the engine block; we bought the wrong filter; the box says it has the right filter but it has the wrong filter in it, etc. I normally only write the two or three things that the volunteer has called out and I ask the students to take note of what I am doing: identifying risks.

I point out that they all thought that the original estimate of 10 minutes was reasonable until I got them to think about things that could go wrong, and now 10 minutes is "scary." I then ask the volunteer how long it could take to change an oil filter if all the things identified that could go wrong did go wrong. The volunteer usually answers that it would take anywhere from half an hour to two hours.

I then tell them about the history of how the U.S. Navy developed the Program Evaluation and Review Technique (PERT)[4] and how you can determine an expected value for your estimate using the PERT mean formula:

$$PERTmean = \frac{O + 4ML + P}{6}$$

Where:

O = The optimistic estimate (in our example, 10 minutes)

ML = The most likely estimate (15 minutes)

P = The pessimistic estimate (120 minutes)

For our example:

$$32 \text{ minutes} = \frac{10 + 4(15) + 120}{6}$$

---

[4]http://en.wikipedia.org/wiki/PERT.

Some people would say that 32 minutes is rather long to use as an estimate for changing an oil filter. I ask how many of them remember when Jiffy-Lube® guaranteed a 10-minute oil change. It's now 30 minutes and guess what was one of the primary problems that drove them to 30 minutes: the oil filter.

The trick to this is that the team member doesn't get 32 minutes to change the oil filter. The prudent project manager will not even tell the team member what the expected value is. The team member only gets 15 minutes—their most likely estimate—to complete the task. The additional 17 minutes goes into a contingency bucket for when things go wrong. If a little thing goes wrong and it takes the team member 20 minutes to complete the work package, then the project manager is still "banking" 12 minutes to use for other Murphys on other work packages. The project manager had better have quite a few minutes from other work packages in this contingency "bank" to make up for the time when everything that can go wrong does go wrong (Murphy) and it takes the full two hours to complete the oil filter change.

I can see the eyes rolling now: "It's hard enough to get one estimate. How can we now ask for four different pieces of information for each work package? Isn't that too much detail?"

Detail that makes the project a more successful endeavor is worth it. Every time I've convinced the project managers I've consulted with or mentored to ask for these four pieces of information instead of a single estimate, they've come back to tell me that it actually made the estimating process easier on the team members involved. When one estimate is requested, the team member frets over the process. They feel that a "gun will be put to their head" if they miss the estimate.

Asking for the four pieces of information allows the team member to identify threats that, if they happen, are outside of their control. The project manager can choose to mitigate these threats by adding tasks that might lower the probability or the impact of the threats if they happen, or the project manager can accept the threats knowing that there is a contingency "bank." The team member is challenged to accomplish the work package within the most likely estimate.

TRANSLATING EFFORT TO THE COST OF A WORK PACKAGE

Let's take a look at what costs money on a project:

- Resources get paid for the work they do that is charged to the project.

- Indirect costs incurred by the organization are "loaded" or "burdened" on the labor rates of the resources.

- Materials that the resources need to accomplish the work are charged to the project.

- Expenses, such as travel, required to accomplish the work are charged to the project.

Many time estimates of work are expressed in working days rather than effort. When this is the case, the number of people or units and the effort involved for each person or unit must be determined to calculate the cost of the work package.

Once the effort of each resource assigned to the work package has been determined, a simple calculation of that effort times each resource's unit costs (sometimes also called a burdened or fully loaded labor rate) can be performed. The unit cost of a resource is commonly calculated using the following formula:

Unit Cost = Base Rate * (1 + Indirect Cost Percentage)

where:

- Base rate is an average planning rate for a particular labor category and

- Indirect cost is a percentage that represents both overhead costs and general and administrative costs (G&A).

This base rate closely represents the amount of money that is paid to the individual resource for each hour expended on the contract. Overhead cost percentage covers all the other costs of doing business, such as vacation time, sick leave, benefits, utilities, building leases, etc. G&A is another percentage for the labor costs associated with upper management and the administrative staff, such as human resources, finance, etc. All the organization's projects are "burdened" by these indirect cost percentages equally or equitably as defined by the cost accounting practices of the finance department.

Once the unit cost of each resource has been determined, the estimated cost of the work package is then calculated using:

$$\text{Cost} = (\text{Effort} \times \text{Unit Cost}_{(resource)}) + \text{Expenses}$$

HOW INDIVIDUAL PRODUCTIVITY IMPACTS THE COST ESTIMATE

In many instances, the best method for obtaining an estimate of effort for a work package is to ask someone who has accomplished this type of work package in the past. We call these people "subject matter experts" (SMEs). Since these SMEs have accomplished the same or similar work before, they shouldn't be using a guess, but will use an analogy (e.g. "the last time I did that it took me X hours"), basing their estimate on one previous experience, or they will have in their mind a parametric (e.g., "on average it takes me X hours").

How we ask for this information is very important. Never ask an SME to estimate how long it will take someone else to do the work package. The SME should be asked to provide the estimate as though they would be doing the work and then the project manager should adjust this estimate based on a comparison of the individuals assigned to the work with the SME's knowledge, skills, attitude, physical/mental strength, etc.

The biggest mistake most project managers make is to "force" an estimate on a project team member. The individual assigned the work has to feel a sense of being able to accomplish the assignment for the proper amount of their productivity to be expended. Project managers who think they can control people in this manner are deluding themselves. Once the individual assigned to the work package senses failure, they will "shrug their shoulders" and slow down because they do not "feel" that they can succeed and the project doesn't matter to them anymore. Their productivity wanes and the probability of the work package being accomplished on time diminishes.

Project managers, as leaders, understand this basic concept and recognize that the "A" in SMART stands for "attainable" or "agreed to." If they get an estimate from an SME, they will adjust it in a realistic manner so that the individual assigned "buys in" to the assignment.

The best technique is to determine a productivity factor for each individual being considered for the work package based on the SME at 100 percent productive. To see how this might be done, let's use the example resource matrix of a small archeological dig project in Table 4-1.

The SME for the first work package in the matrix would probably be Lee, since all the university libraries are probably in his bookmarks/favorites on his web browser. Let's say that Lee says it might take him 80 hours of effort to accomplish this research task. This now gives us a "base" to use for adjusting each resource being considered for this task; this means that Lee

Work Package	Resource	Kim No experience, but has a shovel Rate: $36/hr	Karen 10 years experience in the field Rate: $77/hr	Lee PhD, Paleontology, from U of Montana Rate: $95/hr
123.05.01 Research dig				
123.05.02.01 Survey area of dig				
123.05.07 Dig				

Table 4-1. Sample Productivity Matrix

would have a productivity factor of 100 percent since he based his estimate on his own knowledge and skill.

We can now consider Karen. She certainly should be able to do the research, but probably not at the same productivity rate as Lee. Let's say that Karen's productivity would be about 75 percent of Lee's. This is a subjective method of determining a productivity factor, but in most project plans individual productivity is never considered at all.

Now we can consider Kim. Some may say that she cannot be assigned to this work package because she has no experience, but research on a wide variety of subjects was a task we all were expected to accomplish in high school or definitely in college, so we should consider her. Also, how often do we get that "warm body" matrixed to our project from a functional department? We often have to consider team member assignments where the knowledge or skill level is weak. Kim might be able to do the research, although definitely not at the same productivity factor as Lee.

Let's say that Kim's productivity factor is subjectively determined to be about 25 percent of Lee's. The one thing to consider beyond her low productivity factor is that Kim could be a great help to whoever is assigned to this task, which would lower the effort required by the original assignee and provide tremendous on-the-job training opportunities to Kim.

I remember at a previous job where I was in charge of a Cost and Schedule Control Department (what would now be called a Project Office) and I brought four project managers together in a meeting to discuss the fact that they were all trying to use the same person on each of their projects, full time, at the same time. They had this poor guy scheduled to work 32 hours a day, every day, for six months.

I was told that they were not going to take the time to get into that kind of detail in planning their projects. This guy was "good" and always "comes through," and he was the only person in the entire company who had the skills they needed.

Well, this guy was "good" all right. If you came to the office at night, he was there. If you came to the office over the weekend, he was there. He was "good" right up until he quit his job and all four of these projects came to a total standstill.

I often thought about what the outcome would have been if they had only gotten him help, even if it was a Kim-type person to do some of the rudimentary tasks that were part of his job. The Kim-type person could have assumed some of the burden and learned a tremendous amount in the process.

Back to our example: Which one of these resources would be able to complete the research tasks for the least cost? Many would think Kim is the answer, since her rate is the lowest, at $36 an hour, compared to Karen's at $77 and Lee's at $95.

The simplest formula for this situation is:

$$\text{Cost}_{(\text{resource})} = \frac{\text{Effort}}{\text{Productivity Factor}} \times \text{Unit Cost}_{(\text{resource})}$$

This means that Lee would cost:

$$\text{Lee}_{(cost)} = \frac{80 \text{ Hours}}{1.00} \times \$95/\text{hr} = \$7,600$$

Karen would cost:

$$\text{Karen}_{(cost)} = \frac{80 \text{ Hours}}{0.75} \times \$77/\text{hr} = \$8,213$$

Kim would cost:

$$\text{Kim}_{(cost)} = \frac{80 \text{ Hours}}{0.25} \times \$36/\text{hr} = \$11,520$$

As you see, Kim is definitely not the least expensive resource for this work package. As a matter of fact, the resource with the highest rate is the one that will cost the least in this example.

Now let's look at the work package "Dig." If we choose Kim as the source of the estimate, she—like so many other resources who are expected to come up with an estimate of how long it will take to complete a work package even though they've never done the work before—may say that her best guess is 80 hours. Since Kim made the estimate based on her own knowledge (or lack thereof) and skills, we have to see her as having the base 100 percent productivity factor and each other consideration will now be compared to Kim.

We can consider Karen, who has 10 years of field experience in archeological digs, for this work package. Comparing Karen to Kim would probably be determined as something like 150 or 200 percent, since Karen has experience and would certainly do a higher quality job on this work package.

We may subsequently decide that Karen would have been a far better person to give us an estimate of the effort for this work package. Once we get the estimate from Karen, we have negated Kim's original estimate and the base productivity factor that goes along with it, and we now use Karen as our 100 percent base productivity factor.

Our resource matrix, with productivity factors entered for each work package, is shown in Table 4-2.

Work Package	Resource	Kim No experience, but has a shovel Rate: $36/hr	Karen 10 years experience in the field Rate: $77/hr	Lee PhD, Paleontology, from U of Montana Rate: $95/hr
123.05.01 Research dig		25% productivity factor	75% productivity factor	80 hours effort estimate 100% productivity factor
123.05.02.01 Survey area of dig		25% productivity factor	40 hours effort estimate 100% productivity factor	90% productivity factor
123.05.07 Dig		50% productivity factor	80 hours effort estimate 100% productivity factor	0% productivity factor

Table 4-2. Resource Matrix with Productivity Factors

If you would like to give this a try, try the exercise on the next page. The answers are on the following page.

Exercise 4-A
TRANSLATING EFFORT INTO COST

Given the following information and the limitation that you can only pick one resource per task, which resource is the best choice based on cost?

$$\text{Cost}_{\text{(resource)}} = \frac{\text{Effort}}{\text{Productivity Factor}} \times \text{Unit Cost}_{\text{(resource)}} + \text{Expenses}$$

	Estimate Effort	John Doe—Unit Cost $65/hr Productivity Factor	Jim Beam—Unit Cost $75/hr Productivity Factor	Mary Smith—Unit Cost $85/hr Productivity Factor	Ann Land—Unit Cost $95/hr Productivity Factor
Task A	80 hours	90%	80%	40%	75%
Task B	88 hours	80%	40%	75%	90%
Task C	120 hours	40%	75%	100%	80%
Task D	40 hours	65%	100%	80%	40%

Solution for Exercise 4-A
TRANSLATING EFFORT INTO COST

	Estimate Effort	John Doe	Jim Beam	Mary Smith	Ann Land
		Cost	Cost	Cost	Cost
Task A	80 hours	$ 5,778	$ 7500	$17,000	$10,133
Task B	88 hours	$ 7,150	$16,500	$ 9,973	$ 9,289
Task C	120 hours	$19,500	$12,000	$10,200	$14,250
Task D	40 hours	$ 4,000	$ 3,000	$ 4,250	$ 9,500

Task A—John Doe is the cheapest

Task B—John Doe is the cheapest

Task C—Mary Smith is the cheapest

Task D—Jim Beam is the cheapest

THE CONTROL ACCOUNT

The level above the work package, which is usually a roll-up of a number of work packages that make up a component part or configuration unit of the overall deliverable, is called a control account or cost account. This is considered a management level where the earned value analysis data will be collected and analyzed. A team member with knowledge of project management, sometimes called a control account manager (CAM), is usually delegated responsibility for the monitoring and reporting of the work completed in their control account during the execution and controlling processes (which will be covered in Part 4).

THE PLANNING PACKAGE

During the initiation process, many of the components of the project scope may have yet to be decomposed, identified, and decided on. This does not need to hold up the planning, execution, and controlling process for those parts of the project scope that have been decomposed and agreed upon. These un-decomposed components can be designated "planning packages." They require a "high-level" or "mid-level" estimate of effort, which in turn is translated into rough estimates of cost and time that are used in the planning process until further decomposition, identification, and decision making take place.

This determination to go forward with the known parts of the project scope, while there are still unknown parts of the scope, must be reached with a full understanding of the risk of doing so and the approval of all stakeholders.

TRANSLATING EFFORT TO DURATION OF A WORK PACKAGE USING AVAILABILITY

For our purposes, we will define duration as workdays, usually expressed in calendar days (e.g., "this will take two weeks or three months"). The calendar day duration is often referred to as elapsed time.

The duration of a work package is determined using the estimate of the effort of that work package, based on the productivity factor of the resource assigned plus the availability factor of that resource. Let's use the previous example of the archeological dig, as shown in Table 4-3.

Work Package	Resource	Kim No experience, but has a shovel Rate: $36/hr	Karen 10 years experience in the field Rate: $77/hr	Lee PhD, Paleontology, from U of Montana Rate: $95/hr
123.05.01 Research dig		25% productivity factor	75% productivity factor	80 hours effort estimate 100% productivity factor
123.05.02.01 Survey area of dig		25% productivity factor	40 hours effort estimate 100% productivity factor	90% productivity factor
123.05.07 Dig		50% productivity factor	80 hours effort estimate 100% productivity factor	0% productivity factor

Table 4-3. Example of Resource Matrix

Let's say that Lee is currently working on three other projects and you are now considering using him for this project. If we assume that his time is equally distributed to each project, at best Lee is available to your project 25 percent of his time (and this presumes that Lee is a machine that can switch his brain from one project to another without missing a beat).

Let's also say that Karen is available 33 percent of her time and Kim is available 50 percent of her time. Our new resource matrix is shown in Table 4-4.

Work Package	Resource	Kim No experience, but has a shovel Rate: $36/hr	Karen 10 years experience in the field Rate: $77/hr	Lee PhD, Paleontology, from U of Montana Rate: $95/hr
123.05.01 Research dig		25% productivity factor 25% availability factor	75% productivity factor 25% availability factor	80 hours effort estimate 100% productivity factor 25% availability factor
123.05.02.01 Survey area of dig		25% productivity factor	40 hours effort estimate 100% productivity factor	90% productivity factor
123.05.07 Dig		50% productivity factor	80 hours effort estimate 100% productivity factor	0% productivity factor

Table 4-4. Resource Matrix with Availability Information

A formula that can be used for determining a workday duration for each resource being considered is the following:

$$\text{Duration}_{(resource)} = \left(\frac{\text{Effort}}{\text{Productivity Factor}} \right) \div \text{Availability Factor} \div \text{Hours/Workday}$$

This then would mean that each of our resources would take the following workdays (assume an 8-hour workday) to complete the research work package:

$$\text{Lee}_{(duration)} = \frac{80 \text{ Hours}}{1.00} \div 0.25 \div 8 \text{ Hrs/day} = 40 \text{ Workdays}$$

$$\text{Karen}_{(duration)} = \frac{80 \text{ Hours}}{0.75} \div 0.33 \div 8 \text{ Hrs/day} = 43.29 \text{ Workdays}$$

$$\text{Kim}_{(duration)} = \frac{80 \text{ Hours}}{0.25} \div 0.5 \div 8 \text{ Hrs/day} = 80 \text{ Workdays}$$

This shows that Lee, even though he is less available for this project in general, will still get this research work package completed in the least amount of time.

The duration of each work package must be realistically determined before the project can be planned properly. Remember, as noted in Chapter 2, it is not so vital that we stay on the plan, but that the plan emulate reality so we can direct this reality back toward the plan. If the duration of each work package is unrealistic, the idea of failure will permeate the project plan.

Try the exercise on the next page. The solution follows it.

Exercise 4-B
TRANSLATING EFFORT TO DURATION

Given the following information and the limitation that you can only pick one resource per task, which resource is the best choice for duration?

$$\text{Duration}_{(resource)} = \left(\frac{\text{Effort}}{\text{Productivity Factor}} \right) \div \text{Availability Factor} \div 8 \text{ Hrs/Day}$$

	Estimate Effort	John Doe—Available 50% Productivity Factor	Jim Beam—Available 33% Productivity Factor	Mary Smith—Available 66% Productivity Factor	Ann Land—Available 25% Productivity Factor
Task A	80 hours	90%	80%	40%	75%
Task B	88 hours	80%	40%	75%	90%
Task C	120 hours	40%	75%	100%	80%
Task D	40 hours	65%	100%	80%	40%

Solution for Exercise 4-B
TRANSLATING EFFORT TO DURATION

	Estimated Effort	John Doe Duration	Jim Beam Duration	Mary Smith Duration	Ann Land Duration
Task A	80 hours	22.25 wd	37.88 wd	37.88 wd	53.33 wd
Task B	88 hours	27.5 wd	83.33 wd	22.22 wd	48.89 wd
Task C	120 hours	75 wd	60.61 wd	22.73 wd	75 wd
Task D	40 hours	15.38 wd	15.15 wd	9.47 wd	50 wd

wd = work day

Task A—John Doe is the quickest

Task B—Mary Smith is the quickest

Task C—Mary Smith is the quickest

Task D—Mary Smith is the quickest

5 BALANCING THE SCOPE TO THE BUDGET

Once the estimated cost of the individual work packages defined in the WBS has been determined, a bottom-up roll-up can be calculated. If the project deliverable level roll-up of the cost estimates is higher than the budget for the deliverable, then either the budget for the deliverable is raised or the parts of the deliverable are removed or lowered in quality. Conversely, if the project deliverable level roll-up of the cost estimates is lower than the budget for the deliverable, then either the budget is lowered or additional parts of the deliverable are added or current parts are enhanced in quality.

The determining factor for which parts should be included in the scope and which parts should be changed or left out completely should be based on what is commonly called a benefit to cost analysis. This analysis determines if quantitative or qualitative benefits result from the costs incurred to complete the work of developing the project deliverable or any part of the project deliverable.

An example of a bottom-up roll-up is shown in Figure 5-1. To really get an idea of how the bottom-up roll-up of the initiating subprocess works, try Exercise 5-A on the following pages. (By the way, there is no correct answer to the exercise.)

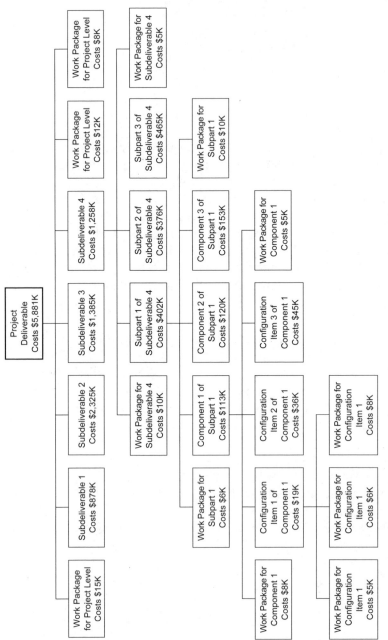

Figure 5-1. Example of Bottom-up Roll-up

Exercise 5-A
BOTTOM-UP ROLL-UP

Your project is to build a backyard pond for your customer. You have spent some time with your customer and have determined that he wants a stone border, a waterfall, some attractive plants, and fish.

You've discovered that for a pond to be an ecosystem, you need to have oxygenating plants, bog plants, floating plants, and snails to eat the algae.

With the information on the next few pages, balance the cost of the work of this project, plus the purchases, to the customer's budget, which is $1,500.

Project Team Members	Charge Rates	Material Costs		Liners	
Supervisor	$75/hour	Plants		Hard-molded Liner	$125.95
Designer	$50/hour	Oxygenating grasses	$4.00/bunch	Soft Liner	$72.95
Buyer	$35/hour			Water Test Kit	$15.95
Tester	$35/hour	Bog Plants			
Skilled Laborer	$25/hour	Cattails	$10.95/plant	Pumps	
Unskilled Laborer	$15/hour	Irises	$23.95/plant	Heavy-duty Pump	$87.95
		Papyrus	$26.95/plant	Regular Pump	$56.95
Work Estimates					
		Floating Plants		Rock	
Major Design	1 hour	Lotus	$67.95/plant	Round River Rock	$298/pallet
Minor Design	1/2 hour	Waterlillies	$46.95/plant	Flat River Rock	$376/pallet
Any Buy	1 hour	Water Hyacinth	$12.95/plant	Flagstone	$496/pallet
Fill Pond	3 hours				
Major Test	1 hour	Fish			
Minor Test/Inspect	1/2 hour	Shabunkins	$8.95/fish		
Minor Installs	10 minutes	Higoi	$22.95/fish		
Install Liner	30 minutes				
Install Border	6 hours	Snails	$5.00/12		
Build Waterfall	2 hours				
Dig Hole	4 hours				

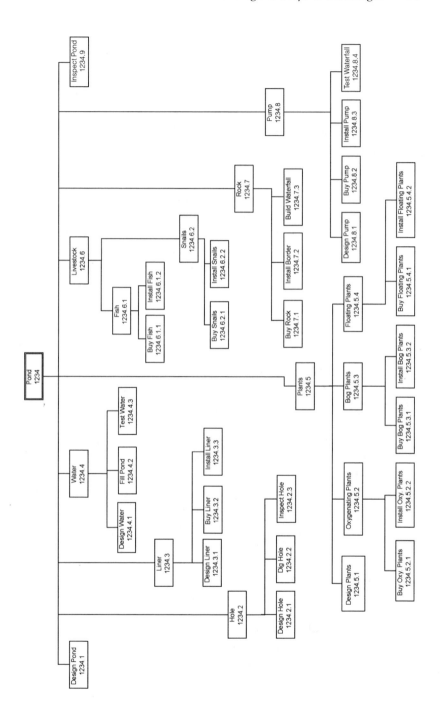

DETERMINING OTHER STAKEHOLDER NEEDS/ WANTS

The customer or user is not the only stakeholder who has needs on the project. Your organization's management has a tremendous amount of need on any project. These needs may fall under the auspices of IEEE, ISO-9000, or CMM® compliance. They tend to come under the category of having standardized processes and documentation. They lend themselves to better communication, quality, and efficiencies. In other words, every complete WBS should include a major category of deliverable known as "project management," broken down into such major deliverable areas as project planning and project control. Project planning encompasses all project management planning deliverables, such as a project management plan and a risk management plan. Project control encompasses such deliverables as the project baseline, the metrics report, and the project status report.

Another major component of most projects is "engineering management," which encompasses such deliverables as the change control process, technical reviews, and quality management.

A third major component of most projects is often referred to as "logistics." Logistics encompasses all the supporting components of the project deliverable, such as training, user documentation, and support equipment.

Also there are work packages on every project that do not equate to a deliverable, such as monitoring and oversight tasks. Often referred to as "level of effort" work packages, these must also have an estimated amount of effort associated with them.

To truly define the work and be able to proceed to the planning process of integrated cost and schedule control, a determination of the "what" of each of these areas (as well as any others) that fulfills stakeholder needs must be included in the overall scope of the project. The effort of each of the work packages defined under these major deliverables must be estimated, translated into a cost estimate, and included in the roll-up of the cost of the scope.

BASELINING THE SCOPE

Once the scope of the project is balanced with the budget and agreed to by the stakeholders, it is a good idea to lock the scope in as a baseline. This lends itself to the first steps of the controlling process because any change to the scope now must go through a change management process. Any of these changes can happen only if there is a change in requirements; since determining and analyzing requirements can be the most volatile part of the initiating process, these changes can easily occur. Using the tools and techniques of the controlling process will assist the project manager in keeping these changes under control.

Now that we have our scope defined and balanced to our budget, let's see how to balance that third side of the triple constraint: time.

PART **3**   THE PLANNING PROCESS

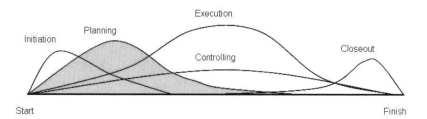

Without a plan, we have no way of measuring progress. Often I've seen project plans presented that were never meant to measure progress, but were instead meant to "check a box" that a project plan was completed. This is what I call "very expensive wallpaper."

Most books available today on the subject of project management state that the WBS is part of the planning process. Actually, only the work packages identified through the decision processes made during initiation, using the WBS, are used in the planning process. The entire WBS comes into play at the end of the planning process only if the deliverable requires descoping as a result of the unavailability of resources to complete all the work defined as the scope during initiation.

The goal of the planning process is to produce a network schedule, to adjust the network schedule to the time the deliverable is needed, and to balance the schedule to the scope to the budget for the triple constraint. This network schedule will show how all the work packages to produce the entire deliverable or any usable segment of the deliverable can be completed on time for the customer to use it. The notion of "on time" will be marked as a "due date" or "deadline." Accomplishing the planning process completes the triple constraint of having the scope identified that fits in the budget and can be accomplished when the customer needs or wants it.

The planning process does not guarantee that the goal will be accomplished, but it does produce the "guidance system," known as the baseline, that will be used during the executing and controlling processes of the project.

Missed due dates or deadlines can cause a variety of problems for your organization, such as:

- Potential loss of revenue

- Loss of competitive edge

- Eroded relationships with stakeholders

- Loss of user credibility

- Possible legal repercussions.

To avoid these types of problems, a thorough understanding of what is involved in developing a network schedule is a required skill of project managers.

The planning process is the easiest of all of the processes once the initiation process does its job of truly identifying all the work packages of the project's scope. However, the steps of this process are the most difficult to grasp for those who are new to the planning process. This is why many project management software tools exist and are so widely used. These tools do most of the steps that you will learn.

So why learn the steps, you may ask, if there are tools to do them for you? Well, if the tool ever makes a mistake (which usually happens because something was not entered properly), you will have no way of knowing until it is too late. Unless you understand the "brain work" behind the tool, you will find it extremely difficult to isolate and find any problems with the plan.

This is why these next few chapters take you through each step involved in project scheduling:

- Understanding workflow and how work packages relate to each other

- Building a network schedule using different methods and techniques

- Analyzing and adjusting the schedule

- Analyzing the schedule for risk

- Readdressing scope to balance the schedule and resources.

6 UNDERSTANDING WORKFLOW AND HOW WORK PACKAGES RELATE

Once the "what" of the project is defined via the initiating process, the "how" must be determined. The identification of the work packages on the WBS can be further broken down into activities (also called tasks) that must be accomplished. Figure 6-1 shows the further decomposition.

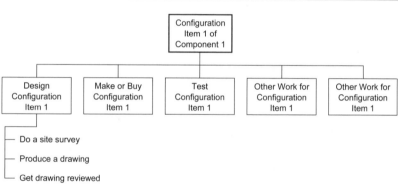

Figure 6-1. Breakdown of Work Package to Activities

Truly understanding the workflow relationship between work packages, activities, or tasks is the first step in developing a network. Activities have a start and a finish. Activities flow in an order. This means that the start or the finish of any activity is dependent on the start or finish of one or more other activities (called the predecessors) and will also drive the start or finish of one or more other activities (called the successors). Figure 6-2 is a simple illustration of this concept.

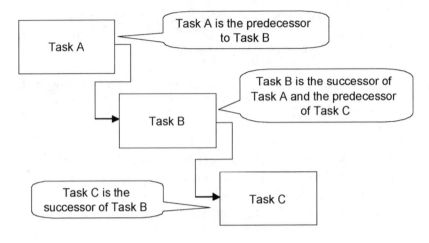

Figure 6-2. Predecessor and Successor Tasks

These relationships between work packages, also known as links, can be expressed in four different ways:

- Finish-to-start

- Start-to-start

- Finish-to-finish

- Start-to-finish.

FINISH-TO-START

The finish-to-start relationship is the most used in network scheduling. It essentially means that the successor cannot (or should not) start until the predecessor has actually finished (see Figure 6-3). There was a time when the various project management software tools required the discipline of these relationships in that they would not allow an actual start date to be entered in the successor (it would just disappear) until an actual finish date was entered in the predecessor. The tools have since "given up" on this discipline because work tends to start when it is able to start, not based on some predefined relationship.

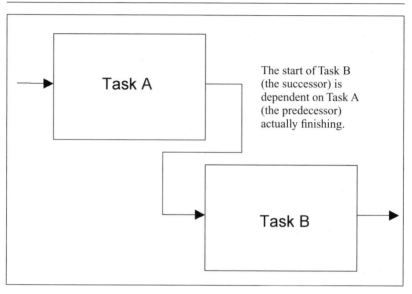

Figure 6-3. Finish-to-Start Relationship

The finish-to-start relationship is best used for those tasks where the start of the successor is truly dependent on the finish of the predecessor; for example, I cannot start painting a wall until the drywall has been installed. If the work of the successor can truly start earlier than the finish of the predecessor, then one of the other relationships should be considered.

START-TO-START

Contrary to what many people believe, the start-to-start relationship does not mean that two tasks start at the same time. The start-to-start relationship means that the start of the successor is dependent on the predecessor actually starting (see Figure 6-4.)

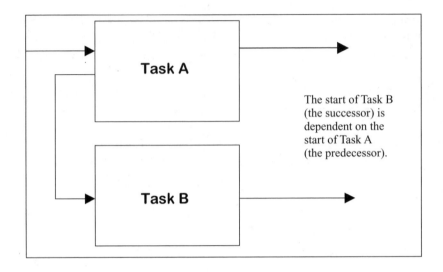

Figure 6-4. Start-to-Start Relationship

An example of a start-to-start relationship is the relationship between writing a document and editing the document. Although you may initially set up these two activities as a finish-to-start relationship, the document does not have to be finished before the editing can begin. Therefore, these two activities can be represented with a start-to-start relationship because the start of editing is dependent on the writing having started and some of the writing of the document having been produced. The start of editing cannot occur before the start of writing; it can occur only after that point.

Note that the finish of Task A must be logically linked to the start or finish of one or more successor tasks. This is done so that any impact of a delay of the finish of Task A will be displayed.

FINISH-TO-FINISH

Again, contrary to popular belief, the finish-to-finish relationship does not mean that two activities will finish at the same time. It means that the successor cannot finish until the predecessor has actually finished (see Figure 6-5.)

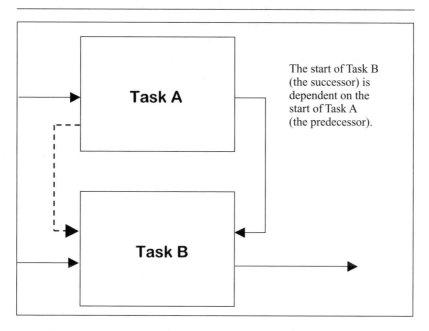

The start of Task B (the successor) is dependent on the start of Task A (the predecessor).

Figure 6-5. Finish-to-Finish Relationship

The relationship between writing a document and editing the document can also be an example of a finish-to-finish relationship because the finish of editing is dependent on the writing of the document finishing.

Note that the start of Task B must have a logical link from one or more predecessors in order to display the impact of this start being delayed. Some project management software programs allow more than one relationship to occur between two tasks. Others, like MSProject®, do not.

START-TO-FINISH

One of the most difficult relationships to understand is the start-to-finish relationship. This is when the start of a task (considered the predecessor because its start drives the relationship) allows the task that has been going on (the successor) to finish (see Figure 6-6).

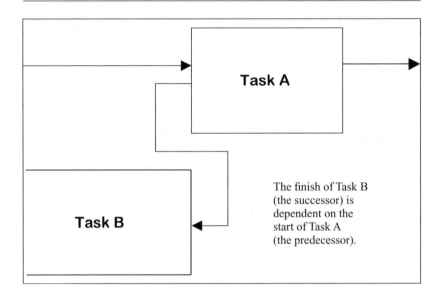

Figure 6-6. Start-to-Finish Relationship

An example of this relationship is when a new system is being built that will replace a currently used system. The start of the use of the new system, which is dependent on an entire network schedule for its development and therefore can be delayed if the development is late, is what allows the old system to be turned off or uninstalled. This keeps the old system from being turned off prematurely.

LAG AND LEAD

There are situations where we may not want the start or the finish of the successor to happen immediately after the start or the finish of the predecessor. For example, we paint a wall and after the painting is complete we hang pictures on the wall; however, there is some time that must go by after we paint the wall to allow the paint to dry. This time is often called "dead" time, in that no labor or material resources are being used. If the painters will be paid for standing around waiting for the paint to dry, the project manager should include this time in the duration of the painting task. If the painters are expected to go do something else while the paint is drying, the project manager may choose to use a "lag."

A lag is time on the "link" between two work packages that delays the successor. In our example, if the paint takes three hours to dry, we may want to use a lag of three hours on the link between the finish of painting the wall to the start of hanging the pictures. Figure 6-7 illustrates this example.

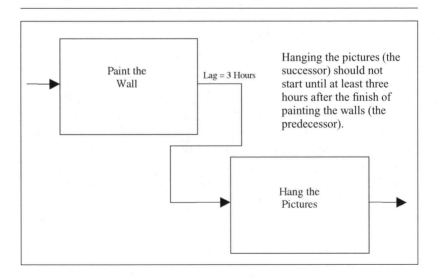

Figure 6-7. Finish-to-Start Relationship with Lag

For our start-to-start relationship example of writing a document and editing a document, the edit work package usually cannot start simultaneously with the start of the writing work package. There needs to be time for some amount of writing to be done before the editing can begin. Figure 6-8 illustrates this lag.

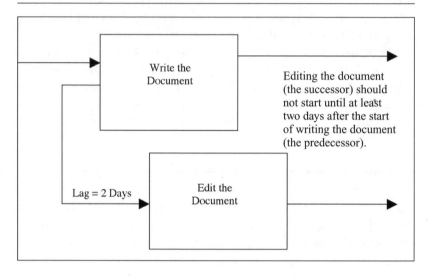

Figure 6-8. Start-to-Start Relationship with Lag

In the finish-to-finish example, the start of the edit work package is allowed to occur whenever there is enough writing to edit; however, rarely is the editing completed at the same time that the writing is completed. This is another example of where a lag would be used to delay the planned completion of the editing work package to a time when we think it truly may be completed. Figure 6-9 illustrates this example.

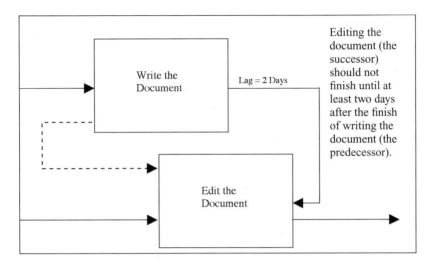

Figure 6-9. Finish-to-Finish Relationship with Lag

For our start-to-finish example, the use of some lag time delays the turning off of the old system for a specified amount of time. This allows the two systems to be run in parallel after the new system is started for however long the project manager decides is needed before the old system is stopped. Figure 6-10 illustrates this example.

Lead, also known as negative lag, allows the start or the finish of the successor (depending on the type of relationship used) to occur earlier than the start or finish of the predecessor. For example, we may want to start the cleanup of a facility one day before the completion of the installation. If the installation is delayed because predecessor work is delayed, the start of the cleanup work package will also be delayed. Figure 6-11 illustrates this example.

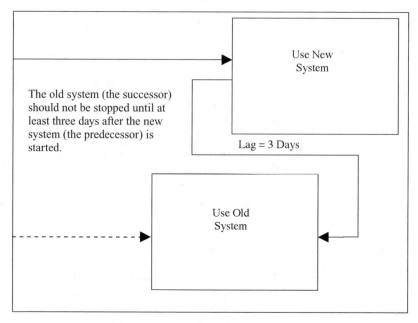

Figure 6-10. Start-to-Finish Relationship with Lag

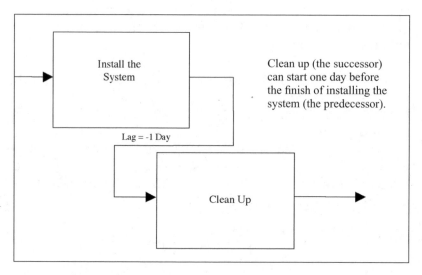

Figure 6-11. Finish-to-Start Relationship with Lead

CONSTRAINTS

Constraints are conditions, or sometimes limitations, that are placed on the work package start or finish. When developing a network schedule, we generally assume that all work packages are going to start "as soon as possible" (determined by the relationship we establish). Constraints should be used sparingly (i.e., only when the plan requires them). A plan that is artificially constrained is unrealistic and amounts to "wallpaper."

A constraint adjusts the work package in the following possible ways:

- *Must start/finish on.* This constraint is the least flexible because it forces the start or finish of a work package to a particular date. The schedule should show the project manager the impact of reality. If the schedule is not flexible, the project manager will be under the false impression that all is well (or not well, depending on the situation). This type of constraint should be used as infrequently as possible and only when the situation requires it.[5]

- *Start/Finish no sooner than.* This constraint alerts the user if the actual start or the actual finish of the work package is earlier than a designated date.

- *Start/Finish no later than.* This constraint alerts the user if the actual start or the actual finish of the work package is later than a designated date.

Now that we have an understanding of how work flows, let's see how a network is actually built.

---

[5]An example of where this constraint was used properly was for Y2K, where the switch from December 31, 1999, to January 1, 2000, was inflexible.

7 BUILDING A NETWORK SCHEDULE

It was in the late 1950s that many of the project management philosophies used today were first recognized and the first scheduling techniques were developed. At that time a few astute gentlemen recognized that the work tasks of a project are dependent on each other and that a "workflow diagram" could be developed to show this. Associating this workflow diagram to the timeline developed by Henry Gantt during the early part of the century allowed the work to be planned so the workers knew when they were expected to start and finish each task. This also gave the project manager a mechanism to oversee the work and manage the impacts of work being accomplished late.

These techniques matured during the early 1960s using various forms of network analysis to develop the methods of network scheduling that are used today. Two of these methods are the arrow diagramming method (ADM) and the more mature precedence diagramming method (PDM.)

Before we explore these two methods, there are certain "rules" that pertain to every network schedule:

- Only the lowest level of each of the branches of the WBS, the work package level, further decomposed activities or tasks, or un-decomposed planning package level should be networked together in the schedule.

- A network can only have one start and one finish. When more than one logically independent network schedule occurs in a project, each individual network needs to have one start and one finish.

- Each work package, task, activity, or planning package must have at least one predecessor to its start, unless it is the one start.

- Each work package, task, activity, or planning package must have at least one successor from its finish, unless it is the one finish.

Many situations will fall into the category of "chicken and egg." For example, is the design of the hole in the pond mentioned in Chapter 3 dependent on the design of the livestock and the plants, or is the design of the livestock and the plants dependent on the design of the hole? Some fish will grow dependent on their environment. If we want large fish, then the design of the hole is dependent on the type of fish we buy and how large we want the fish to grow. If we do not care about the fish growing, then the type of fish we buy is dependent on the design of the hole.

It is critical to have your entire team assembled to assist in putting together the network schedule. You want input from the team so that you, as the project manager, can make the final decision. This goes back to our basic concept of success. If the team has input into the decision, they can more willingly accept the notion of it possibly being the wrong decision and will provide further input to help resolve the issue. If you make the decision with no input from the team, and it turns out to be a wrong decision, the team may wonder why the decision was made in the first place and you will lose credibility as a leader.

NETWORK SCHEDULING USING THE ARROW DIAGRAMMING METHOD

Many students ask why we would even address arrow diagramming methods when hardly anyone uses it anymore. I usually answer them with "That's not true."

Sprint Corporation

One of the best uses of arrow diagramming methods I've seen was instituted at the Sprint Corporation back in the 1990s. An employee decided that he could get the upper levels of management at Sprint to use project management techniques to express their strategic visions of where the company should be in 5–10 years. He used an arrow diagram, networking what projects would be needed to get them there. He then had the Graphics Department draw the project diagrams in such a way that they could be displayed on the walls throughout the company's headquarters.

This accomplished a number of very positive things: It showed each project team member how their project fit into the strategic vision of the company; it allowed good decision making concerning if and when to terminate a project that no longer fit into the strategic vision of the company; and, better yet, it provided a discipline to the company's upper management that they could not just change their mind on a whim, but would have to map out any new vision and show how the ongoing projects would fit into this new vision.

The only down side to this was that because upper management used what they refer to as "task on arrow," all the project managers assumed that they were to use the same network diagramming method. ADM works best when there are only a few work packages (in Sprint's case, projects) that are being networked together.

Let's see why this is. First of all, ADM, also known as activity on arrow (AOA) or task on arrow (TOA), was the first network scheduling technique developed back in the late 1950s by an employee at DuPont Industries. Before that time, the concept of linking the completion of one project activity as a predecessor to allow the start of another project activity in a network was not recognized. ADM allowed for networking and display of all project activities. This was then used to show how the work of the project was to be performed and how much time the project might take to complete. Using ADM, all the information about an activity or work package is displayed on the arrow (see Figure 7-1).

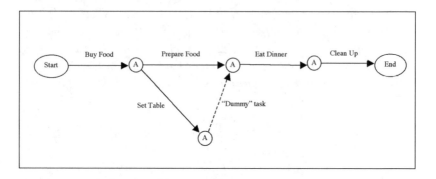

Figure 7-1. Example Network Schedule Using ADM

This method can display workflow to a completion time, but it has a few limiting features:

- ADM can only display the relationship between two work packages as a finish-to-start relationship, which is limiting and often unrealistic.

- Using the arrows in ADM to display the work package information requires the use of a "dummy arrow" to show some relationships.

To illustrate a network schedule using ADM, let's look at the six work packages of a small wallpapering project in Table 7-1.

Work Package	Duration
Buy Wallpaper	4 Hours
Buy Supplies	2 Hours
Cut Wallpaper	3 Hours
Prepare Walls	8 Hours
Hang Wallpaper	12 Hours
Clean Up	2 Hours

Table 7-1. Work Packages for Wallpaper Hanging Example Project

If I were the only resource doing this wallpaper project, the network schedule would be one arrow after the other, because I can only do one thing at a time. Even though I can go to the same store to buy the wallpaper and the supplies, I can only do one of those work packages at any given time.

If I have help, however, the network schedule may look like Figure 7-2.

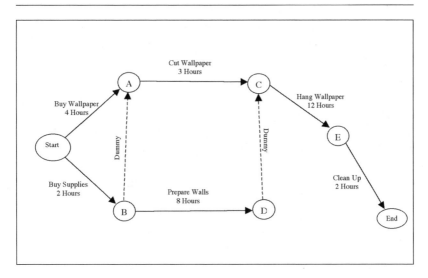

Figure 7-2. Example Arrow Diagram

Because I have help, buying the wallpaper can happen at the same time as buying the supplies. Cutting the wallpaper is dependent on having bought the wallpaper, but also on having bought supplies with which to cut the wallpaper. This is where a "dummy" activity comes into play. I could place the start of the "cut wallpaper" activity on the finish of the "buy wallpaper" activity, but there also needs to be a "dummy" arrow going from the finish of the "buy supplies" activity to the start of the "cut wallpaper" activity.

The "prepare walls" activity is dependent only on the "buy supplies" activity. The "hang wallpaper" activity is dependent on having the wallpaper cut but also on having the walls prepared. This requires another "dummy" activity going from the finish of the "prepare walls" activity to the start of the "hang wallpaper" activity. The "clean up" activity is dependent only on having the wallpaper hung, and it is the last activity, so it goes to the end.

In this example, there are two "dummy" arrows. In a large, complex project, with many interdependencies, this method would get very messy and would not be the best method to use. However, for smaller projects or to strategize at the higher levels of a large project, this method is easiest and works quite well.

In the early 1960s the U.S. Navy began to use this arrow diagramming technique for their many projects. They discovered that work flows in what they called "paths" from the start of the project to the end. The longest path gave them the duration of the project, which they could report to their superiors. This longest path was dubbed "the critical path" because, if the work on this path was not completed as planned, the projected completion date could be missed. The Navy also began to perform more analysis of the critical path, using what they called the Program Evaluation and Review Technique (PERT, introduced in Chapter 4 and discussed further in Chapter 9), to determine the probability of meeting the project completion date.

Today, the concept of the critical path is widely misunderstood by many who call themselves project managers. *The critical path has nothing to do with the critical work of the project.* As a matter of fact, the critical path has its own inherent risk, in that it is the path of work that could cause the scheduled end date to be missed. It would seem that the prudent project manager would try to keep the critical work of the project *off* the critical path.

The critical path is not the only path of work that has to be managed. As we will see with an example of our next diagramming method, if the noncritical paths of the schedule are ignored, the project could be doomed to failure.

The critical path is the longest path through the network schedule and, therefore, determines the duration of the schedule. It is the path (and there can be more than one critical path) of the work that must be completed as planned if the completion dates of the project are to be met. (As we will see in Chapter 8, there are techniques that can be used to change the critical path as needed.)

Looking back at our example arrow diagram in Figure 7-2, three paths reach from the start of the project to the end of the project. Each of these must be analyzed to determine which one is the longest path (i.e., the critical path.) Figures 7-3, 7-4, and 7-5 show the three paths and how long it would take to do only the work on each.

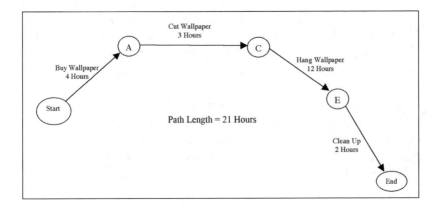

Figure 7-3. First Path through Arrow Diagram

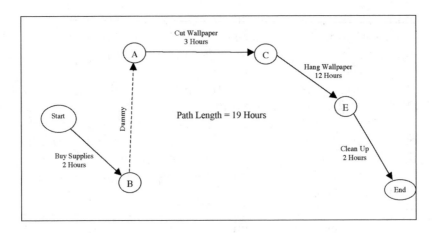

Figure 7-4. Second Path through Arrow Diagram

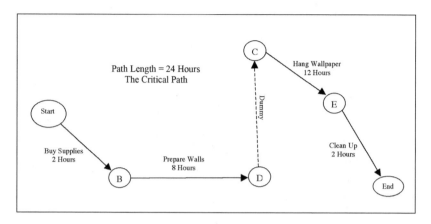

Figure 7-5. Third Path through Arrow Diagram

The third path (Figure 7-5) is the longest and therefore the critical path, which tells us that the project will require 24 working hours to complete with the network schedule that we have now.

To see if you can pick out the paths and determine which one is the critical path, try Exercise 7-A.

Exercise 7-A
ARROW DIAGRAMMING METHOD

In the arrow diagram below: How many paths are there? Which path is the longest (i.e., the critical path)?

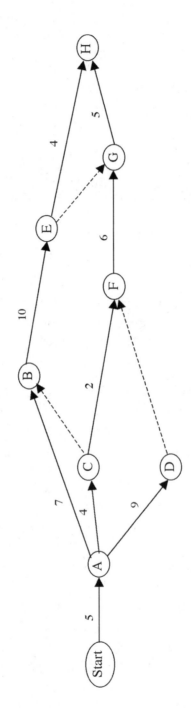

Solution for Exercise 7-A
ARROW DIAGRAMMING
METHOD

There are six paths:

Start -> A -> B -> E -> H

Start -> A -> B -> E -> G -> H

Start -> A -> C -> B -> E -> H

Start -> A -> C -> B -> E -> G -> H

Start -> A -> C -> F -> G -> H

Start -> A -> D -> F -> G -> H

The longest is:

Start -> A -> B -> E -> G -> H = 27

NETWORK SCHEDULING USING THE PRECEDENCE DIAGRAMMING METHOD

Because the arrow diagramming method only allows finish-to-start relationships and uses "dummy" activities, it became obvious to the early developers of network scheduling techniques that this method does not work as well for large, complex projects; thus, the advent of the precedence diagramming method (PDM). Also known as activity on node (AON), PDM puts the information about the activity on the node of the network and, because it uses the arrows only to show relationships, it allows all four of the task relationships to be displayed.

This method is far more conducive to team collaboration and the use of the Post-it® notes used in building the WBS. Only the work package Post-it® notes at the bottom of any branch of our WBS are put in the network schedule, and the facilitator can place each Post-it® note in the network as the team describes. Let's use the wallpaper example to demonstrate this method. If we assume that there is just one resource, Figure 7-6 shows a possible PDM network.

It can be argued whether to buy the wallpaper before the supplies or the other way around. This is an example of the "chicken and egg" dilemma. If a team member believes that one way is best, he or she should be allowed to express an opinion. If the team as a whole overrides an individual team member's opinion, that team member will tend to accept the team's decision even though he or she may not agree with it.

On the other hand, if the project manager makes all the decisions without letting the team members express their opinions, the team will tend to be less productive on the project, especially if they feel that the decision was the wrong one. The project managers who have the most successful projects encourage their teams to express their opinions throughout both the initiating and the planning subprocesses.

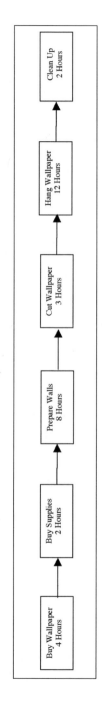

Figure 7-6. Example Precedence Diagram

There is a big difference between working time and calendar time. Our full calendar day is a combination of both working time and non-working time; we need to identify both to understand the work being done over time. Project management software tools also must be "educated" as to what we mean by working and non-working time if they are to accomplish the analysis of the network schedule and be able to produce the information we need to manage the project.

For example, let's assume that I would like to do this wallpaper project over a weekend, starting Saturday morning. Now, I'm an early riser who likes to do her yoga in the dark. I try to start any project by 8:00 a.m., and I have plans to go out to dinner with friends on Saturday night, so I want to stop working at 6:00 p.m. I'll get up and go to an early church service on Sunday and be able to start work by 8:00 a.m. Sunday is clear for the rest of the day for me to continue to work as long as I need to in order to finish the job, but I do have to go to work on Monday.

To identify the time that each work package can start and finish, we will need to perform what is called a "forward pass" and place the notation of this early start/finish time on the upper corners of our Post-it® note box. Performing a forward pass enables us to identify the earliest time that each work package can start based on the relationship it has with its predecessor(s). (A detailed explanation of the steps of the techniques used in this example will be presented in Chapter 8.)

Figure 7-7 displays a forward pass on our wallpapering project network schedule as we currently have it. Note that our start time is 8:00 a.m. on Saturday.

Since the duration of our first work package, "buy wallpaper," is four hours, the earliest it can finish is noon. Because there is a finish-to-start relationship between "buy wallpaper" and "buy supplies," the earliest time that our "buy supplies" work package can start is noon. Since the duration of "buy supplies" is two hours, the earliest we can finish this work package

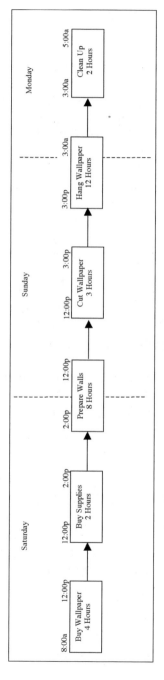

Figure 7-7. Example Precedence Diagram with Forward Pass

is 2:00 p.m.; the earliest we can start the "prepare walls" work package is also 2:00 p.m.

The duration of the "prepare walls" work package is longer than the rest of the working time that is left for Saturday (remember, I want to stop at 6:00 p.m. to get ready to go out to dinner with friends). This means that four of the eight working hours required to prepare the walls can be done on Saturday and the other four working hours will begin at 8:00 a.m. and finish at noon on Sunday. The forward pass then continues through the rest of the network until we find the earliest time that the last work package, "clean up," can finish.

As you see, I can get the job done in time to jump in the shower and prepare for work, but I probably am not going to be very productive at my job because I got very little sleep Sunday night. Since being productive at my job is a much higher priority than having a wallpaper project completed, I must decide if I should cancel or try to find another resource to help me get the project completed sooner.

If I can find additional resources, I can then redo my precedence diagram and perform a new forward pass to see if I can develop a more realistic planned schedule for my project. Redoing the network schedule to get the work accomplished sooner is called "compressing the network schedule."

COMPRESSING OUR EXAMPLE SCHEDULE

According to the *PMBOK*®, schedule compression is "shortening the project schedule without reducing the project scope, to meet schedule constraints, imposed dates, or other schedule objectives." Two techniques used to achieve schedule compression are "fast tracking" and "crashing."

Fast tracking is the rescheduling of activities that would normally be planned to be completed in series, one after the other in a finish-to-start relationship, to be accomplished in parallel. For the full compression to be realized, if the same resource is assigned to the activity being rescheduled in parallel, then a new resource would need to be found who can accomplish the work with the same productivity as the original resource.

Some think that this addition of resources will end up doubling the cost of the project, but it normally does not. Let's add some costs to our example to see if this is true. We will do this as simply as we can by assuming that my unit cost is $100 per hour. As can be seen in Figure 7-8, the total costs for the project would be estimated as $3,100.

Let's now see if we can get some work planned to be completed in parallel, understanding that this will require additional resources.

As seen in our arrow diagram of the previous section and also as shown in Figure 7-9, we can plan for one resource to buy the wallpaper while another resource buys the supplies. This allows both work packages to begin at the start of the project. The cutting of the wallpaper is dependent on both the wallpaper having been bought and the supplies with which to cut it having been bought. Preparing the walls is dependent only on the supplies having been bought. Hanging the wallpaper is dependent on both the wallpaper having been cut and the walls having been prepared. Once the hanging of the wallpaper is finished, we can clean up.

The total estimated cost of the project remains at $3,100. This is because the activities of buying and cutting the wallpaper were taken away from the original resource (i.e., $700 worth of work is no longer assigned to the original resource) and are now assigned to the new resource.

Our new forward pass is shown in Figure 7-10.

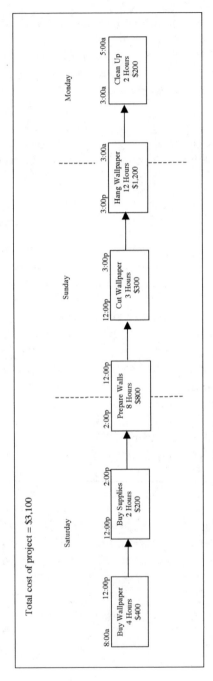

Figure 7-8. Example Precedence Diagram with Estimated Costs

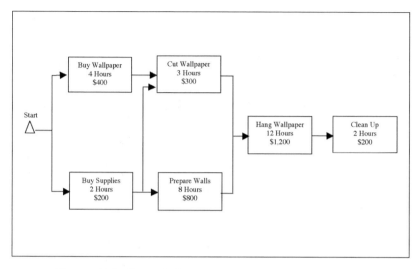

Figure 7-9. Example Precedence Diagram Compressed

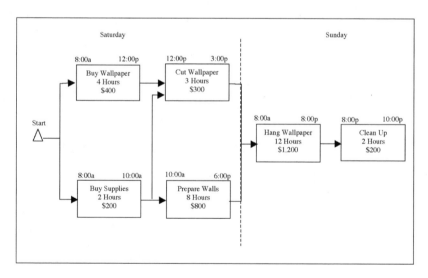

Figure 7-10. Example Precedence Diagram Compressed with
Forward Pass

Notice that the "cut wallpaper" work package is dependent on both the wallpaper being bought and the supplies being bought (i.e., it must wait until both of these work packages are completed). Of the two, the work package that takes longer is "buy wallpaper." So, the earliest time that "cut wallpaper" can start is the earliest time that "buy wallpaper" can finish, i.e., noon.

"Hang wallpaper" is another example of a work package that is dependent on two predecessor work packages (cut wallpaper and prepare walls) being completed before it can start. Since the "prepare walls" work package takes the longest and the earliest that it can finish is 6:00 p.m., which is when I want to stop working on Saturday. This means that the earliest the "hang wallpaper" work package can start is 8:00 a.m. on Sunday.

Completing the forward pass on my network schedule determines that the earliest I can complete my entire project is 10:00 p.m. on Sunday. I can live with that and still get a good night's sleep to be productive at my job on Monday morning. With more resources, I could probably get the project done more quickly, but why overuse resources if the end time meets my objectives of getting the job completed in a weekend, having dinner with my friends on Saturday, and being productive at work Monday morning? As currently planned, my project needs only one additional resource on Saturday from 8:00 a.m. until 3:00 p.m. and at no extra charge, assuming their rate is the same as mine!

Now that I know the end time for my project, I can further analyze the network schedule to determine how much flexibility there is related to when each work package "can" start and when each "must" start. To do this I will perform what is called a "backward pass" and note these late start/finish times in the lower corners of my Post-it® notes box. The backward pass identifies the latest time that any task must start and finish.

The backward pass starts at the end time of the entire network schedule, which was determined based on the early finish of the last work package while performing the forward pass. The analysis for the backward pass uses a disciplined "must" mode. An example of this disciplined thinking, when all work packages have finish-to-start relationships, is the following: If the last work package is to finish at a particular time, when is the latest it must start, based on its duration? For this work package to start at this late start time, all of its predecessors must be finished by that time or before, so what is the latest that each predecessor must finish? The technique continues to work backward to try to determine when each work package must finish, and based on its duration must subsequently start, until all the work packages have a late finish and a late start.

The backward pass in our example (see Figure 7-11) starts with the "clean up" work package and identifies the latest we want that work package to finish as 10:00 p.m. Going backward, the latest that this two-hour work package must start to meet the 10:00 p.m. finish time is 8:00 p.m. For that to happen, all of the predecessors of the "clean up" work package must be finished by 8:00 p.m., or sooner.

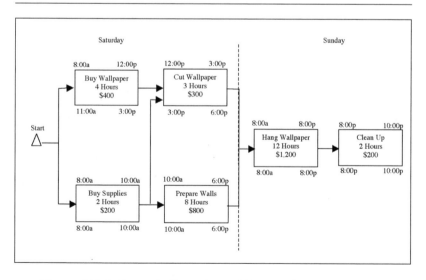

Figure 7-11. Example Precedence Diagram Compressed with Backward Pass

The predecessor of the "clean up" work package is the "hang wallpaper" work package. Before we can determine the late finish of the "hang wallpaper" work package, we must first see if it is a predecessor to any other work package in the network. If it is a predecessor to more than one work package, we would need to determine the successor work package that has the earlier of the late starts and get the "hang wallpaper" work package done in time for that successor, which would subsequently have it finished in time for the other successor work packages' late start.

Because the "hang wallpaper" work package is not a predecessor to any other work package, the only criterion for the "hang wallpaper" work package is to get it done in time for the "clean up" work package's late start (i.e., 8:00 p.m.). Therefore, the late finish for the "hang wallpaper" work package is 8:00 p.m., which in turn means, because the duration of the "hang wallpaper" work package is 12 hours, that the latest I must start hanging the wallpaper is 8:00 a.m. For this 8:00 a.m. start to happen, all the predecessors of the "hang wallpaper" work package must be finished no later than 6:00 p.m. on Saturday.

The "prepare walls" work package is a predecessor to only the "hang wallpaper" work package, which means that it must finish by 6:00 p.m. Saturday and, because it has a duration of eight hours, it must start at 10:00 a.m. The "cut wallpaper" work package is a predecessor to only the "hang wallpaper" work package, which means that it must finish by 6:00 p.m. Saturday and, because it has a duration of three hours, it must start at 3:00 p.m. The "buy wallpaper" work package is a predecessor to only the "cut wallpaper" work package, which means that it must finish by 3:00 p.m. Saturday and, because it has a duration of four hours, it must start at 11:00 a.m.

The "buy supplies" work package, however, is the predecessor to both the "cut wallpaper" work package and the "prepare walls" work package. This means that to determine the latest time that the "buy supplies" work package must finish, we need to determine which of its two successor work packages has the earlier late start. The "cut wallpaper" work package's late start is 3:00 p.m. The "prepare walls" work package's late start is 10:00 a.m., which is the earlier of the two. This means that the "buy supplies" work package must finish no later than 10:00 a.m., which is in time for both of its successor work packages' late starts. Because it has a duration of two hours, the "buy supplies" work package must start at 8:00 a.m.

The forward pass identified the early start and early finish for each work package. The backward pass identified the late start and late finish for each work package. The difference between the late start and the early start, or the late finish and the early finish, tell us how much time a work package can be rescheduled before the end time of the network schedule, 10:00 p.m. on Sunday in our example, can no longer be successfully accomplished. This time is referred to as "total float" or "total slack."

Total float is calculated for each work package individually. If this difference in time is zero, then the work package is on a critical path, which gives us another definition for the critical path. If this difference is negative, than the work package is considered "critically late" and the network schedule end time will not be successfully accomplished unless some replanning of the schedule is performed.

Note that total float does not refer to different amounts of float being added together as the total float of the project. A project does not have any total float because the duration of the project is determined by the critical path, which has no flexibility.

Figure 7-12 displays the total float of each work package and the critical path.

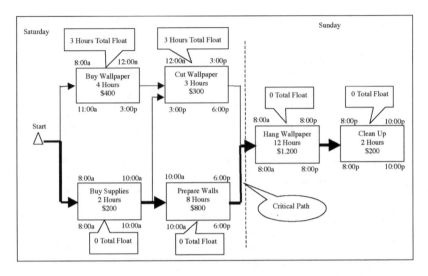

Figure 7-12. Example Showing Total Float and Critical Path

Too often project managers say that once they know the critical path, they have identified the only path to which they need to pay attention. Let's take a look at our example and one scenario that may cast doubt on this notion.

The total float for the "buy wallpaper" work package is three hours (late start of 11:00 a.m minus the early start of 8:00 a.m.) and the total float of the "cut wallpaper" is three hours (late start of 3:00 p.m. minus the early start of 12:00 noon). Neither of these work packages is on the critical path.

The "buy wallpaper" work package can start as early as 8:00 a.m., but the latest it must start is 11:00 a.m. If we assign the "buy wallpaper" work package to someone who likes to sleep in on Saturdays, they might not want to start that work package until the latest it must start, 11:00 a.m. The unenlightened would think that, since there are three hours of total float in this work package, this would not pose a problem. Well, let's see.

Let's say that we also have assigned the "cut wallpaper" work package to a resource who comes from a wallpaper-cutting department. This resource might be assigned to multiple projects that have wallpaper-cutting work packages. Let's say, for example, that they are assigned to Project X to cut wallpaper from 8:00 a.m. to 11:00 a.m. They break for lunch before they come to our house at noon to accomplish our wallpaper-cutting work package, after which they are assigned to Project Y to start cutting wallpaper at 3:00 p.m. The wallpaper-cutting resource now has a full day of work scheduled.

Under this circumstance we could have a wallpaper-cutting resource show up at our house on time at noon, but we have no wallpaper to cut. This not only changes our plan, but we would need to pay this resource for the time that they are standing around and getting absolutely nothing done. Then at 3:00 p.m., when the resource who was assigned to buy the wallpaper shows up with an armful of wallpaper, a very difficult decision has to be made (and we usually expect our resources to make this decision): Does the wallpaper-cutting resource stay and cut our wallpaper or does this resource go to Project Y as assigned? The former decision would keep our project on track, but may have a detrimental impact on Project Y. The latter decision would cause our project to come to a dead stop.

This situation could have been avoided by using another piece of important information that can be calculated from our forward and backward pass data and that might have alerted us before we made any adjustments to our schedule. This is the calculation of how much of the total float time the work package can slip before it impacts another work package. This is commonly referred to as "free float" or "free slack." For a finish-to-start relationship with a successor, the free float is the difference between the early start of the successor and the early finish of the work package that we are analyzing.

Had we calculated the free float of the "buy wallpaper" work package, we would have found it to be zero (early start of the successor, "cut wallpaper" = noon, minus the early finish of work package being analyzed = noon). This means that the buying of the wallpaper cannot be delayed at all from its early start without impacting the "cut wallpaper" work package. In this case that impact could be detrimental to the entire project because we would need a resource that may no longer be available and, worse yet, we would have been paying for this resource's time when absolutely nothing was accomplished.

Now let's say that the manager of the Wallpaper-Cutting Department approaches us and asks if it would be okay for their wallpaper-cutting resource to work on Project X in the morning, work on Project Y from noon to 2:00 p.m., and then come to our house at 2:00 p.m. to cut our wallpaper. We would need to look for the successor to the "cut wallpaper" work package, which is the "hang wallpaper" work package. The early start of the "hang wallpaper" work package is 8:00 a.m. on Sunday, which is synonymous with 6:00 p.m. on Saturday, because we do this calculation using working time only. We would need to subtract the early finish of the "cut wallpaper" work package, which is 3:00 p.m. We would find that all of the total float of the "cut wallpaper" work package is free to us, which means that this work package can be delayed without any impact on any other work package in our network schedule.

If we delay the start of the "cut wallpaper" work package to 2:00 p.m., the earliest it can finish now is 5:00 p.m. Its total float would now be one hour, and that one hour is still free to us. Plus, we have now freed up two of the three hours of total float of the "buy wallpaper" work package. The resource who likes to sleep in can now delay the start of the "buy wallpaper" work package to 10:00 a.m. with no impact on the rest of the network schedule.

Figure 7-13 shows our wallpaper example with the free float information added.

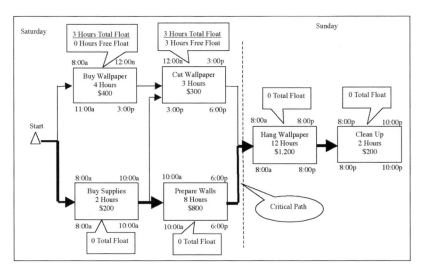

Figure 7-13. Forward Pass and Backward Pass on the Wallpaper Example with Total Float, Free Float, and Critical Path

PLANNING OUR EXAMPLE RESOURCES

Understanding our resource needs is another very important part of developing a network schedule. Our previous analysis shows that we could not have planned to have the project completed by 10:00 p.m. on Sunday unless we were able to get an additional resource to take over the two work packages "buy wallpaper" and "cut wallpaper" on Saturday. The resource profile of my project is displayed in Figure 7-14, which shows that I need two resources between 8:00 a.m. and 3:00 p.m. on Saturday.

Now looking for ways to compress the schedule even more, we could change the relationships of the work packages to have work done in parallel. We would start by recognizing that the "hang wallpaper" work package does not need to wait for all

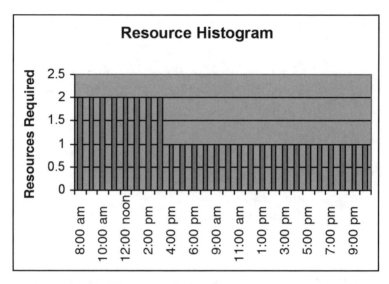

Figure 7-14. Example Resource Histogram

the walls to be prepared and for all the wallpaper to be cut. We could change the finish-to-start relationship between these work packages to a start-to-start, with a lag, that allows enough time for some walls to be prepared (let's say two hours) and the wallpaper to be cut (let's say one hour) to be able to start hanging the wallpaper.

Our network diagram would change to look like the one displayed in Figure 7-15.

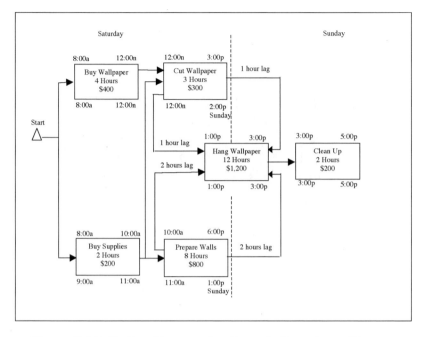

Figure 7-15. Further Compressing Example Precedence Diagram Using Fast Tracking

This allows us to finish the entire project by 5:00 p.m. on Sunday.

Our resource histogram will look like Figure 7-16.

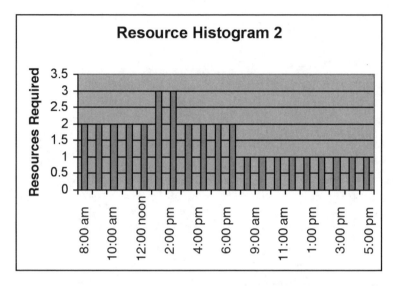

Figure 7-16. Example Resource Histogram 2

If 5:00 p.m. on Sunday is still later than we want this project to take, we have many other solutions that will help compress the project duration. For example, if the wallpapering is being done in two distinctly different areas, we could cut that work package in half, assign each half to a different resource at no additional cost, and compress the schedule as shown in Figure 7-17.

Our resource histogram now looks like Figure 7-18.

COMPRESSING OUR EXAMPLE EVEN MORE

The other schedule compression technique that we can use is "crashing." Crashing involves assigning additional resources to an individual work package to get it accomplished sooner. This has to be done realistically or it may not work. For instance, if an additional resource were assigned to the "buy wallpaper" work package, it might cause that work package to take longer to be accomplished since the two resources might have differing

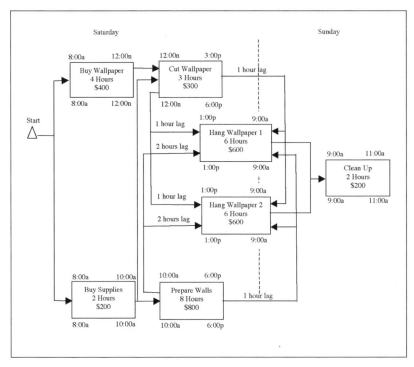

Figure 7-17. More Compression of Example Precedence Diagram Using Fast Tracking

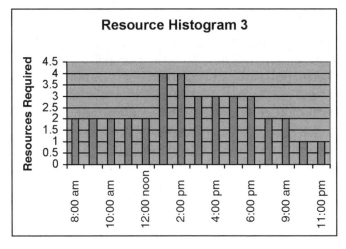

Figure 7-18. Example Resource Histogram 3

ideas on which is the best wallpaper to buy. However, in our example, we might choose to assign an additional resource to each "hang wallpaper" work package. This would not necessarily cut the duration of these work packages in half, but it might reduce the duration from six hours each to four hours each, which would in turn add costs for each resource working an additional hour (i.e., two resources working four hours each at $100 an hour equals $800 per work package.) With this adjustment, our total project cost rises to $3,500 for labor.

We would also need to compress our "prepare walls" work package, because it is now taking longer than the "hang wallpaper" work package.

We can get the "prepare walls" work package accomplished sooner by adding a resource to that work package, and this may cut the duration in half. We could also add a resource to the "clean up" work package, which might reduce its duration by half. Our final schedule would look like Figure 7-19.

Note that all of the work is scheduled to be accomplished by 6:00 p.m. on Saturday. The number of resources we need to be able to accomplish this is shown in Figure 7-20.

Did we spend more money to compress our network schedule from an essentially three-day project to a shortened one-day project? You bet. We now need to plan to pay $3,500 for just the labor, versus the original estimate of $3,100, plus any additional supply costs.

Is the added cost worth the time compression? Only the customer, who is paying for the project, or the sponsor, whose budget is paying for the project, can make that decision. This is what is known as a time/cost tradeoff analysis.

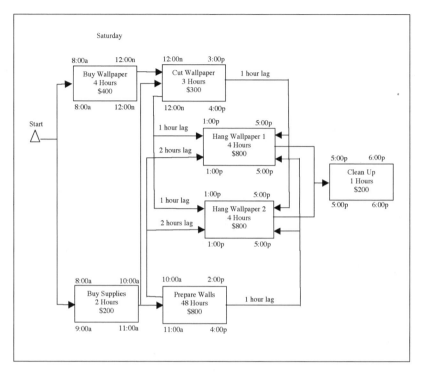

Figure 7-19. Final Compression of Example Precedence Diagram

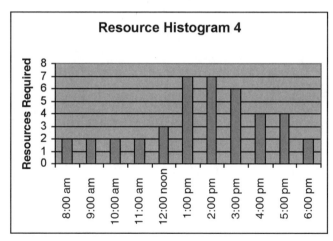

Figure 7-20. Resource Histogram of Final Compression

8 ANALYZING AND ADJUSTING THE SCHEDULE

In the wallpaper example in Chapter 7, we saw how some of the schedule analysis and adjusting techniques work. Now let's take a closer look at each of those techniques.

FORWARD PASS

Again, the forward pass identifies the earliest time that a work package can start and finish. Arguments can be made for starting the forward pass with the first day, week, or month, or "time zero," all of which produce the same results for analysis of the network diagram. I like starting with time zero, simply because it is easier to do.

If we start with time zero, the steps of the forward pass through a finish-to-start relationship are:

1. Start with zero.

2. Add the duration to get the early finish of the task.

3. Recognize that the early start of each successor task will be the latest early finish of each of its predecessor's tasks.

4. Repeat steps 2 and 3 until you find the early finish of the last work package or the end milestone.

Figure 8-1 displays the first three steps.

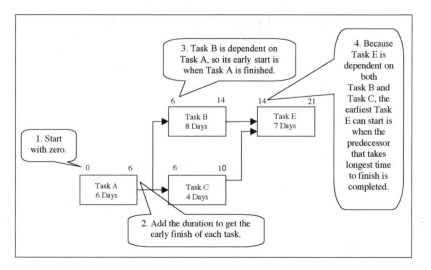

Figure 8-1. Forward-Pass Steps Starting at Time Zero

If we start with day 1, the steps of the forward pass through a finish-to-start relationship are:

1. Start with 1.

2. Add the duration and subtract 1 to get the early finish of the task.

3. Recognize that the early start of each successor task will be the latest early finish, plus 1, of each of its predecessor's tasks.

4. Repeat steps 2 and 3 until you find the early finish of the last work package or the end milestone.

Figure 8-2 displays the first three steps.

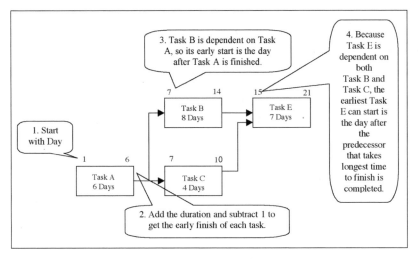

Figure 8-2. Forward-Pass Steps Starting with Day 1

Note that both examples end on the same day.

Figure 8-3 is an example of the forward pass through a finish-to-start relationship network, using time zero as the start, carried through to the end task of the network.

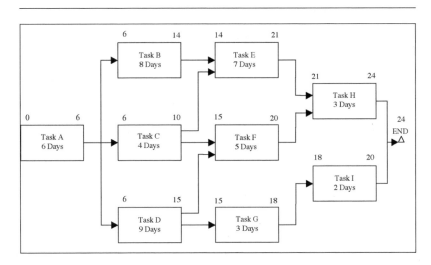

Figure 8-3. Forward-Pass Example Starting with Time Zero

Figure 8-4 is an example of the forward pass through a finish-to-start relationship network, using day 1 as the start, carried through to the end task of the network.

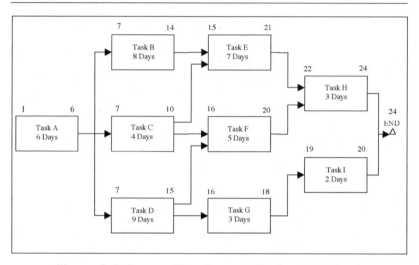

Figure 8-4. Forward-Pass Example Starting with Day 1

BACKWARD PASS

Again, the backward pass identifies the latest a work package can start and finish. The steps of the backward pass through a finish-to-start relationship that uses time zero at the start are as follows:

1. Set the latest early finish, found during the forward pass, of the end of the network as the late finish of each predecessor task that has "end" as a successor. If the end of the network is a work package, then set that work package's early finish as its late finish.

2. Subtract the duration to find the late start of each task.

3. Recognize that the late finish of the predecessor task will be the earliest of the late starts of each of its successor tasks.

4. Repeat steps 2 and 3 until you have zero as the late finish of the start milestone, or the late start of the starting work package.

Figure 8-5 shows the backward pass steps through a finish-to-start relationship when we start with time zero.

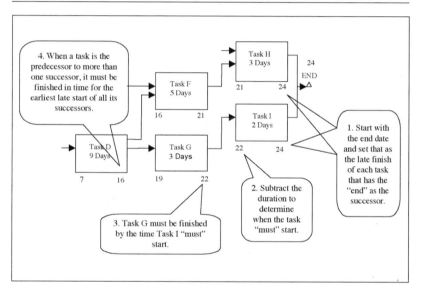

Figure 8-5. Backward-Pass Steps Using Time Zero

If we start our forward pass with day one, the steps of the backward pass through a finish-to-start relationship will be:

1. Set the early finish, found during the forward pass, of the end of the network as the late finish of each predecessor task that has "end" as a successor. If the end of the network is a work package, then set that work package's early finish as its late finish.

2. Subtract the duration and add 1 to find the late start of each task.

3. Recognize that the late finish of the predecessor task will be the earliest of each late start of its successor tasks, minus 1.

4. Repeat steps 2 and 3 until you have 1 as the late finish of the start milestone, or the late start of the starting work package.

Figure 8-6 shows the backward pass steps through a finish-to-start relationship when we start with day 1.

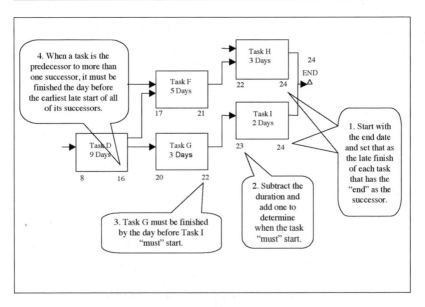

Figure 8-6. Backward-Pass Steps Using Day 1

Figure 8-7 is an example of the backward pass through an entire finish-to-start network, using time zero, carried through to the start task.

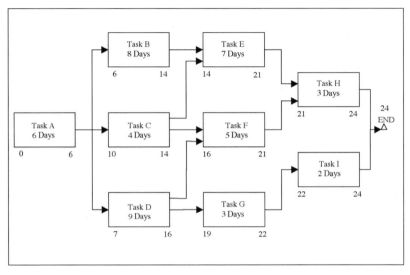

Figure 8-7. Backward-Pass Example Using Time Zero

Figure 8-8 is an example of the backward pass through an entire finish-to-start network, using day 1, carried through to the start task.

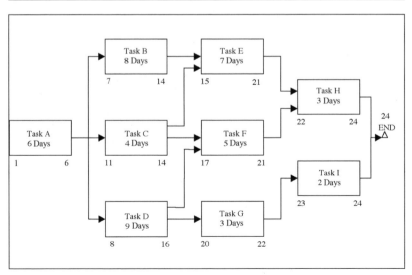

Figure 8-8. Backward-Pass Example Using Day 1

CALCULATING FLOAT

Float (also known as total float, total slack, or slack) is calculated for each work package individually. Contrary to what many people believe, there is no such thing as how much float a project has. Float is the time a work package can be delayed without delaying the end time of the project. It is calculated using one of the following equations (whichever is less):

Total Float = Late Start – Early Start

or

Total Float = Late Finish – Early Finish

Figure 8-9 displays our time-zero example showing the total float for each work package.

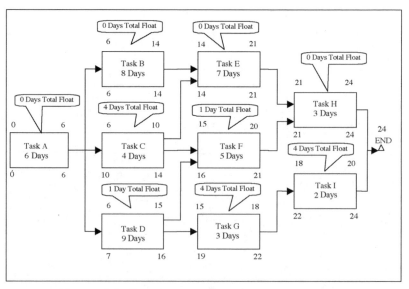

Figure 8-9. Time-Zero Example Showing Total Float

IDENTIFYING THE CRITICAL PATH

Looking back to our example, we notice that there is a path made up of four work packages that all have zero total float. This is another method for finding the critical path, defined as that path (there will always be at least one but there can be more than one) that has work packages that have zero total float.

To recap, the critical path is all of the following:

- The longest path(s) through the network schedule

- The determinant of the overall duration of the project as planned (i.e., the shortest time to complete the project as planned)

- The path(s) with tasks that have zero float

- Not the only path of work requiring management control.

Figure 8-10 displays our time-zero example with the critical path indicated in bold.

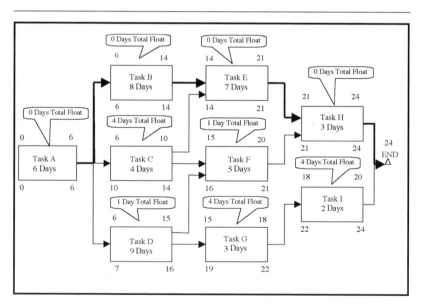

Figure 8-10. *Time-Zero Example with Critical Path*

CALCULATING FREE FLOAT

Free float (also known as free slack) is a subset of total float. As seen in our wallpaper example in Chapter 7, free float is a far more useful piece of information than total float in that it is the amount of time a work package can be delayed before impacting any other work package in the network schedule. The way free float is calculated is highly dependent on the relationship of the work package being analyzed with its successors.

If we use the time-zero start in our forward pass through a finish-to-start relationship, the calculation of free float is as follows:

Free Float = Early Start$_J$ – Early Finish$_I$

Where:

J = the successor

I = the task being analyzed

If there is more than one successor, the minimum difference will equal the free float for the task.

Figure 8-11 displays our time-zero example showing how much of the total float is free to each work package.

If we use day 1 as the start in our forward pass through a finish-to-start relationship, the calculation of free float is slightly different, but it will have the same result as the time-zero method. The formula is as follows:

Free Float = Early Start$_J$ – 1 – Early Finish$_I$

Where:

J = the successor

I = the task being analyzed

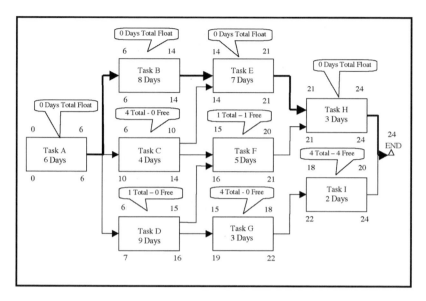

Figure 8-11. Time-Zero Example Displaying How Much of Total Float Is Free

If there is more than one successor, the minimum difference will equal the free float for the task.

If you would like to try this on your own, complete Exercise 8-A on the next page. The answer (using a time-zero start) is on the following page.

Exercise 8-A
PRECEDENCE DIAGRAMMING METHOD: FINISH-TO-START RELATIONSHIPS

In the diagram below, do a forward and backward pass, calculate total float and free float, and mark the critical path.

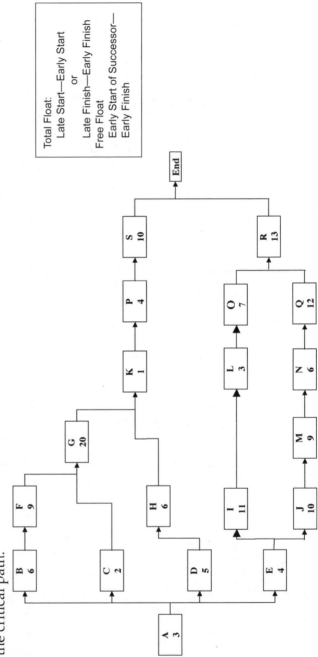

Total Float:
Late Start—Early Start
or
Late Finish—Early Finish
Free Float
Early Start of Successor—
Early Finish

Solution for Exercise 8-A
PRECEDENCE DIAGRAMMING METHOD: FINISH-TO-START RELATIONSHIPS USING TIME-ZERO METHOD

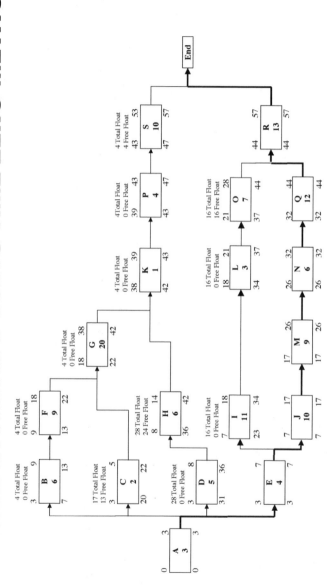

FORWARD AND BACKWARD PASS WITH START-TO-START RELATIONSHIP

Because the start-to-start relationship flows only through the starts, the forward and backward pass of this relationship flows only through the starts also. The steps are the same whether we use the time-zero method at the start or the day-1 method at the start. To make this more interesting, let's include lag on the link between the tasks.

To perform the forward pass, all we need to remember is that the early start of the successor of the start-to-start relationship is the early start of its predecessor, plus any lag.

Figure 8-12 shows the steps of the forward pass through a start-to-start relationship:

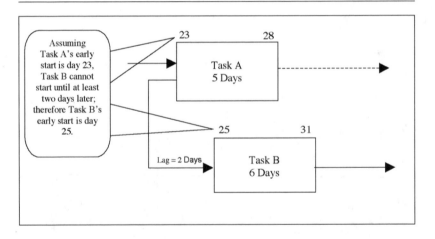

Figure 8-12. Forward Pass through Start-to-Start Relationship

To perform the backward pass, all we need to remember is that the late start of the predecessor of the start-to-start relationship is the late start of its successor, minus any lag.

Figure 8-13 shows the steps of the backward pass through a start-to-start relationship.

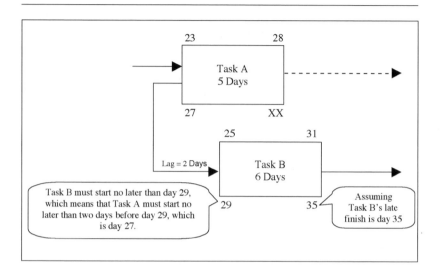

Figure 8-13. Backward Pass through Start-to-Start Relationship

Calculating total float for the work packages on a start-to-start relationship is no different from calculating total float on the finish-to-start relationship. However, the amount of the total float that is free is found using a different approach.

Let's look at calculating the free float of a work package that has a start-to-start relationship with its successor. The formula is the same for both time zero and day 1 used as the start:

Free Float = Early Start$_J$ – Early Start$_I$

Where:

J = the successor

I = the task being analyzed

If there is more than one successor, the minimum difference will equal the free float for the task.

FORWARD AND BACKWARD PASS WITH FINISH-TO-FINISH RELATIONSHIP

Because the finish-to-finish relationship flows only through the finishes, the forward and backward pass flows only through the finishes also.

To perform the forward pass, all we need to remember is that the late finish of the successor of the finish-to-finish relationship is the late finish of its predecessor, minus any lag.

Figure 8-14 shows the steps of the forward pass with a finish-to-finish relationship:

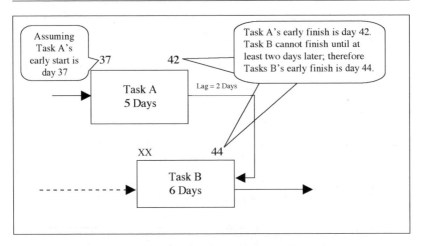

Figure 8-14. Forward Pass, Using Time-Zero Method, through Finish-to-Finish Relationship

To perform the backward pass, all we need to remember is that the late finish of the predecessor of the finish-to-finish relationship is the late finish of its successor, minus any lag.

Figure 8-15 shows the steps of the backward pass with a finish-to-finish relationship.

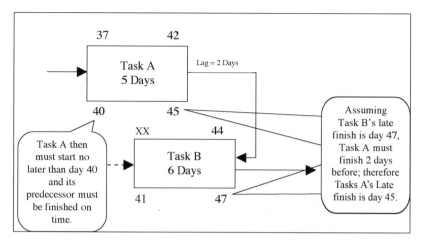

Figure 8-15. Backward Pass, Using Time-Zero Method, through Finish-to-Finish Relationship

---

Calculating total float for the work packages on a finish-to-finish relationship is no different from calculating total float on the finish-to-start relationship. However, the amount of the total float that is free is found using a different approach.

For a finish-to-finish relationship, the calculation of free float would again be the same for both the time-zero and day-1 methods:

Free Float = Early Finish$_J$ – Early Finish$_I$

Where:

J = the successor

I = the task being analyzed

If there is more than one successor, the minimum difference will equal the free float for the task.

Try the exercise on the next page.

Exercise 8-B
PRECEDENCE DIAGRAMMING METHOD WITH OTHER RELATIONSHIPS

In the diagram below, redo the forward and backward pass and mark the new critical path.

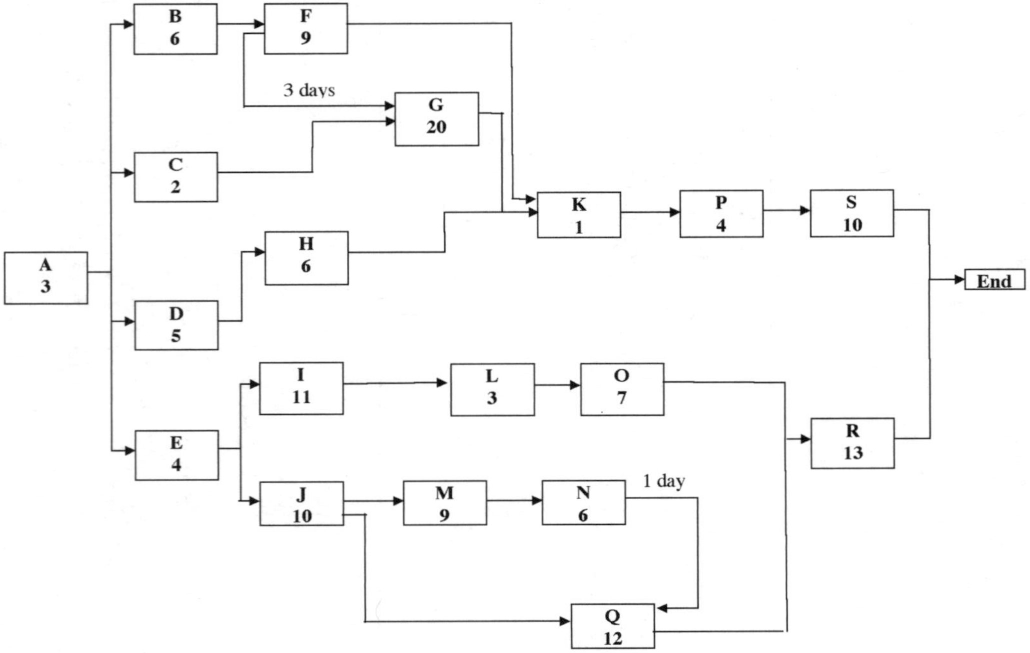

Total Float:
Late Start—Early Start
or
Late Finish—Early Finish
Free Float
For F→S
Early Start of Successor—
Early Finish
For S→S
Early Start of Successor—
Early Start
For F→F
Early Finish of Successor—
Early Finish

Solution for Exercise 8-B
PRECEDENCE DIAGRAMMING METHOD WITH OTHER RELATIONSHIPS

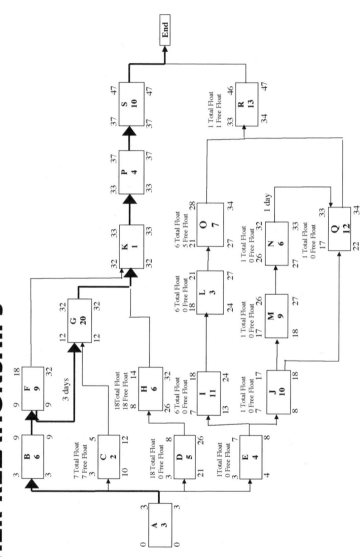

COMPRESSING THE NETWORK SCHEDULE

The goal of the network schedule is not just to meet the date the project is due to the customer, but to beat the date the project is due. This "cushion" of time between the end of our network schedule and the due date falls in the category of "management reserve" for the unknown, unidentifiable risks that happen to all projects. This should not be viewed as "padding" the schedule. Padding is time that the project team gets and will use under normal circumstances; reserve is time that the team does not get to use unless an unidentifiable in-scope risk arises for the project. As we will address in Chapter 9, the real goal is to increase the probability of success of meeting the project's due date, which in turn goes back to our basic concept of everyone wanting to be part of a successful project.

As shown in our wallpaper example in Chapter 7, the two basic techniques of compressing our network schedule are:

- Crashing individual work packages on the critical path

- Fast tracking work packages on the critical path.

Crashing an individual work package can be accomplished by either adding human resources or equipment resources that will reduce the duration of the work package, or by reassigning the work package to a resource that can accomplish the effort of the work package more efficiently. Finding a better, more efficient resource can sometimes be cheaper. In most cases, however, adding resources increases the cost of the work package because two resources rarely can get an amount of work done in half the time as one.[6]

As shown in our wallpaper example, the "hang wallpaper" work package was reduced, but because using two resources

---

[6]For a good discussion of this in the software industry, see Frederick Brooke, *The Mythical Man-Month* (Addison-Wesley), 1975.

would not cut the duration of that work package in half, additional costs for effort and supplies had to be worked into the total project cost estimate.

Fast tracking is the process of getting work that originally was planned to be completed in series (i.e., using finish-to-start relationships) to now be completed in parallel. One method of accomplishing this is by changing the relationship between two work packages or two subflows of work packages originally linked in a finish-to-start relationship to either a start-to-start or a finish-to-finish relationship. Fast tracking can also be accomplished by breaking the work package down into smaller work packages that can then be scheduled to be completed in parallel.

Either approach can be accomplished only if the resources required to perform the work are not now expected to expend an unreasonable amount of effort in their workday. If the resource is expected to work more than a reasonable amount in his or her workday, the expected productivity will be lower and the compression will not be accomplished. This overutilization of resources must be identified and reconciled if the schedule is to be compressed effectively.

RESOLVING RESOURCE CONFLICT

Resource conflict occurs when an individual resource on the project is assigned to expend either more effort than is reasonable in a workday or less effort than will fill his or her workday. This overutilization or underutilization of resources usually occurs in two situations:

- A resource is totally overutilized

- A resource is overutilized during a particular time period and then underutilized during a subsequent time period.

Resource-leveling techniques can resolve the latter situation, but the former situation can only be resolved by adding resources to the plan. Without proper resource planning, the likelihood of project success will be extremely low.

Resource leveling is the rescheduling of work packages from the time period in which the resource is overutilized to a time period in which the resource is underutilized. This can be accomplished by letting the project management software tool automatically level the project; the tool will reschedule work packages using either its default criteria or user-defined criteria, which can entail a number of heuristic algorithms of what to consider first, second, and so on. The project management software tools can level the schedule with the project due date constrained, which may still show overutilization of many resources, or it can level all resources down to no more than the number of predefined hours of effort for the workday and allow the end date of the project to adjust to a date that culminates from the leveling process.

There's a big warning here: Always save your file to another name before letting the software tool automatically level the schedule. Most software tools will show this warning before the leveling process takes place. For a complex schedule, the number of calculations and adjustments made to the schedule are too numerous to recompute in an "undo" command and rarely will be able to reverse to the original state of the schedule before the leveling took place. If the results of the leveling process are not acceptable to the user, the original state of the file may no longer be available.

Leveling can, and most times should, be accomplished manually. The steps involved in leveling resources manually are:

1. Identify the work packages scheduled during the overutilized timeframe.

2. Determine whether any of these work packages have enough total float to be rescheduled to the timeframe where the resource is underutilized.

3. If the total float is also free, reschedule the work package.

4. If the total float is not free, perform further analysis of the utilization of the resources of the impacted successor work packages before rescheduling the work package being analyzed.

5. If no leveling techniques can resolve the situation, acquire an additional resource.

As the steps of this manual process indicate, the best information to display about the work packages being considered is the amount of total float and free float with which each has to work. Only those work packages that have enough free float to resolve the overutilization situation can be rescheduled without having an impact on or conflict with other resources.

This may seem like a lot of work, but it is necessary to resolve resource issues, which tend to cause the most damage in accomplishing any project plan. If the resource feels that they are being overscheduled to the point where they cannot be successful, they will slow down and their productivity will decrease. Also, if a resource works a lot of overtime, other issues (e.g., health, quality) may come into play, adversely affecting the project's success.

Figure 8-16 presents an example of a resource histogram that shows some resource conflict. Figure 8-17 displays the same data in tabular form.

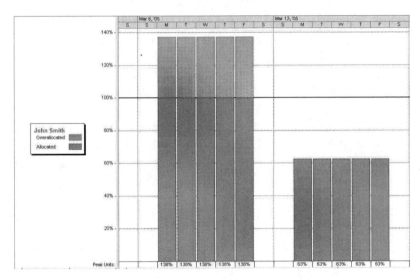

Figure 8-16. Resource Histogram Showing Resource Conflict

ID		Resource Name	Details	05						Mar 13, '05					
				M	T	W	T	F	S	S	M	T	W	T	F	S
35	35	– John Smith	Work	11h	11h	11h	11h	11h			5h	5h	5h	5h	5h
	5	Develop TRP 3.0	Work												
	62	Develop AS 5.0	Work												
	133	Develop COTP 2.0	Work	2h	2h	2h	2h	2h			0h	0h	0h	0h	0h
	189	Prepare for/Participate in Program Office ‍	Work	1h	1h	1h	1h	1h			0h	0h	0h	0h	0h
	207	Conduct Systems Engineering	Work	0h	0h	0h	0h	0h			0h	0h	0h	0h	0h
	236	Develop TSP 2.0	Work	0h	0h	0h	0h	0h			0h	0h	0h	0h	0h
	246	Develop CCP Revision	Work												
	315	Prepare for/Participate in Systems Analysi	Work	1h	1h	1h	1h	1h			1h	1h	1h	1h	1h
	318	Prepare for/Participate in Systems Analysi	Work	4h	4h	4h	4h	4h			4h	4h	4h	4h	4h
	326	Develop/Conduct Systems Analysis and D	Work												
	329	Prepare for/Conduct Systems Requiremen	Work	3h	3h	3h	3h	3h							
	333	Prepare for/Conduct System Design Revie	Work												
	376	Finalize Draft Contract Downselect Plan (‍	Work												
	380	Conduct Systems Analysis and Design Do‍	Work												

Figure 8-17. Table Showing Resource Conflict

As the figures show, the tabular form displays information about the tasks. Information having to do with total float and free float can be added to the table. For example, if work package 329 has both total float of five or more days and free float of five or more days, rescheduling this work package to the following week would resolve the conflict.

Take a look at the resource leveling example in Exercise 8-C.

Exercise 8-C
RESOURCE LEVELING

Mary is assigned to work four hours per day on each of Tasks A, B, C, D, and E.

Mary's resource profile shows that she is both overutilized and underutilized. Using the information provided, choose the task that should be rescheduled to level Mary's task assignments to require no more than eight hours per day of work, yet accomplish all the work by day 9.

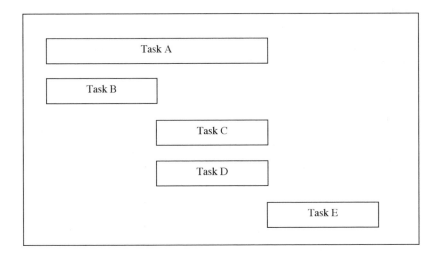

Mary's Resource Profile

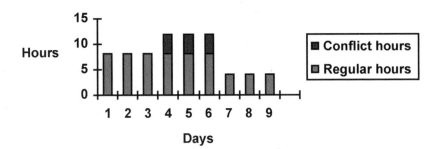

TASK AND RESOURCE INFORMATION

Task Name	Early Start	Early Finish	Total Float	Float
Task A	Day 1	Day 6	0 days	0 days
Task B	Day 1	Day 3	3 days	0 days
Task C	Day 4	Day 6	5 days	0 days
Task D	Day 4	Day 6	3 days	3 days
Task E	Day 7	Day 9	3 days	2 days

Solution for Exercise 8-C
RESOURCE LEVELING

Task D, because it is scheduled to be completed during the overutilization time period, has three days of total float and three days of free float.

Now that we have learned the techniques of analyzing and adjusting our network schedule, let's take a look at how to analyze the risk of our schedule and determine the probability of its success.

9 **ANALYZING SCHEDULE RISK**

If the critical path is not the only path we need to manage, we may ask: What is the use of the critical path? The most important use of the critical path relates to the concept of risk management. By virtue of being the path (or paths) of work packages that have no float, the critical path involves an inherent schedule risk. At the very least, we should check to see what work falls on the critical path. If the critical path happens to run through some of our riskiest work, our probability of success is reduced. To increase our probability of success, we should remove the risky work packages from the critical path using the schedule compression techniques described in Chapter 8.

ANALYZING THE CRITICAL PATH USING PERT

The Program Evaluation and Review Technique (PERT) was devised in 1958 by the U.S. Department of Defense's Navy Special Projects Office as part of the Polaris mobile submarine launch project, which was a direct response to the Sputnik crisis. PERT is basically a statistical summation method of analyzing the work packages along the critical path to determine the probability of success of completing the project given the current network schedule.

PERT is often criticized because it does not consider the summation of the probabilities of the noncritical paths where they merge with the critical path. For project managers who do not analyze their critical path at all using any method, PERT is a great, simple-to-understand place to start.

The basis for a PERT analysis is to have estimates for work packages based on four pieces of information (as discussed in Chapter 4):

- A most likely estimate for completing the work package

- An estimate for completing the work package if everything goes perfectly (the optimistic estimate)

- Two or three things that could go wrong while completing the work package (risk identification)

- How long it would take to complete the work package if all these things do go wrong (the pessimistic estimate)

Once we have these four pieces of information for each work package, the PERT formula to determine the PERT mean is:

$$\text{PERT Mean} = \frac{O + 4ML + P}{6}$$

Where:

O = optimistic estimate

ML = most likely estimate

P = pessimistic estimate

Another piece of statistical information that we need to perform this PERT analysis is the standard deviation of each work package. The formula for the PERT standard deviation is:

$$\text{PERT Standard Deviation} = \frac{P - O}{6}$$

The real analysis that takes place here comes from the basics of statistical analysis. Generally speaking, the reason we use statistics is to be able to make more precise decisions. We do this by gathering as much data as we can, plotting the data, and hoping that our plot will emulate a statistical distribution that has been identified and used in the past. If we can find a distribution in the statistics books that is close to what we plotted, we can use the two magic formulas of the mean and the standard deviation to "normalize" our data. We can then use the normal curve and the analytical assumptions made by Carl Friedrich Gauss, an early 19th-century German mathematician, to determine many things that will help us make decisions.

The way a normal distribution works is that it has the mean as the center point and it forms a bell with curves on each side of the center point mean, the width of which is determined by the standard deviation. According to Gauss, 68 percent of the data collected in the statistical analysis falls within one standard deviation of the mean. Since our network schedule is expressed in time, another way of stating what Gauss assumed is to say that 68 percent of the time our completion date will be within one standard deviation of the mean time.

An illustration will help explain this concept better. Figure 9-1 depicts a standard deviation range.

A large standard deviation will give us a wide range of time, whereas a small standard deviation will give us a smaller range of time. As a result, the standard deviation's size can be used to compare the degree of risk that one work package has to another. In other words, having a 68 percent chance of getting a work package completed sometime within 10 days of our calculated mean time shows us a far riskier situation than if we have a 68 percent chance of getting the work package completed within one day of our calculated mean time. Our confidence in the work being completed on time in the former example is much lower than in the latter example.

The normal curve's shape also changes depending on the size of the standard deviation, as shown in Figure 9-2.

Gauss also determined the amount of data under the normal curve based on multiples of the standard deviation. According to Gauss, a little more than 95 percent of the data collected

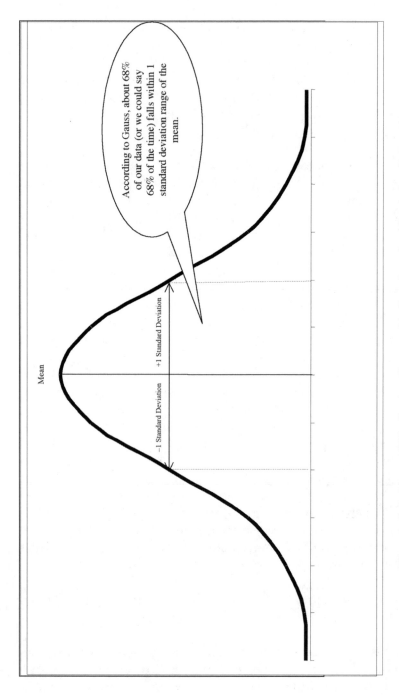

Figure 9-1. Normal Distribution Curve with One Standard Deviation Range

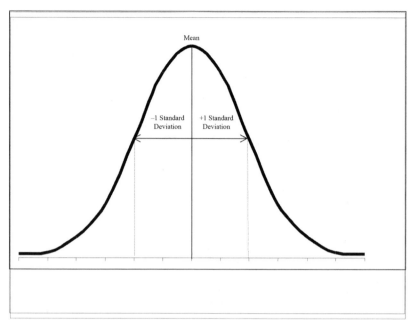

Figure 9-2. Narrower Normal Distribution Curve

would fall within the range (in our case, the range of time) encompassed by two times the standard deviation on either side of the center point mean. A little more than 99 percent of the data collected would fall within the range (in our case, the range of time) encompassed by three times the standard deviation on either side of the center point mean.

Figure 9-3 shows the second and third standard deviation range around the mean.

The developers of the PERT analysis process determined that using the statistical sum theory of statistics on the work packages that made up the critical path would yield a mean and a standard deviation of the duration of the project. Then, by using the Gaussian curve, they could determine the probability of

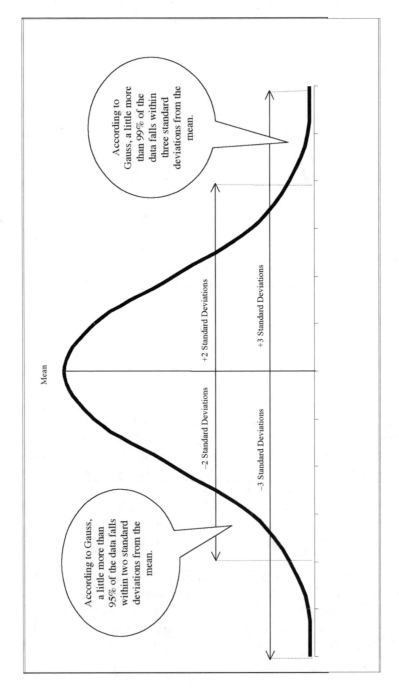

Figure 9-3. Normal Distribution Curve with Two and Three Standard Deviation Ranges

completing the project by a particular date. These developers of PERT used the following formulas:

$$\text{Mean}_{\text{project}} = \sum \text{Means}_{\text{Critical Work Packages}}$$

$$\text{Std.Dev.}_{\text{project}} = \sqrt{\sum \left(\text{Std.Dev.}_{\text{Critical Work Packages}}\right)^2}$$

Let's try this with a simple example. Let's assume that our critical path has five work packages and that our data look like the data in Table 9-1.

Table 9-1. Sample Project Data for PERT Analysis

WPs	Optimistic	Likely	Risks	Pessimistic	(o+4ml+p)/6	(p-o)/6	((p-o)/6)²
A	8.0	10.0		20.0	11.3	2.0	4.0
B	5.0	7.0		15.0	8.0	1.7	2.8
C	20.0	25.0		40.0	26.7	3.3	11.1
D	2.0	3.0		8.0	3.7	1.0	1.0
E	5.0	10.0		25.0	11.7	3.3	11.1
Project		55.0		Mean =	61.3	Σ((p-o)/6)² =	30.0
						SQRTΣ((p-o)/6)² =	5.5

To illustrate how we calculated the data in the last three columns:

$$\text{Task A Mean} = \frac{8 + 4(10) + 20}{6} = 11.3$$

$$\text{Task A Stand Dev} = \frac{20 - 8}{6} = 2$$

$$(\text{Task A Stand Dev})^2 = 2 * 2 = 4$$

For the project level:

$$\text{Mean}_{\text{project}} = 11.3 + 8.0 + 26.7 + 3.7 + 11.7 = 61.3$$

$$\text{Std.Dev.}_{\text{project}} = \sqrt{4 + 2.8 + 11.1 + 1.0 + 11.1}$$

$$\text{Std.Dev.}_{\text{project}} = \sqrt{30.0}$$

$$\text{Std.Dev.}_{\text{project}} = 5.5$$

Our project mean is 61.3 (let's use "days") and our standard deviation, which was found by taking the square root of the sum of the squares of our five work package standard deviations, is 5.5 days. Figure 9-4 shows the normal curve using our data (using "σ" as a symbol for standard deviation).

This does not complete our analysis because the ranges Gauss provided can also be used to calculate the confidence, or probability-of-success, scale. To do this we need to recognize our "x" axis (along the bottom) as a timescale and accept that there is a time way to the left, say day 20, by which we pretty much have a 0 percent change of getting the five work packages completed, and that there is a time to the right, say day 90, by which we have very close to a 100 percent chance of completing the work.

The mean always has a 50 percent chance. That is, you can be 50 percent confident that the five work packages can be completed by the time of the mean or sooner. In our example, we would have a 50 percent chance of completing our five work packages by day 61.3 or sooner.

You may think that 50 percent is not very good, but remember that we used the individual means of the work packages on the critical path to calculate the project mean. They each have a 50 percent chance using their means, and 50 percent of the time they'll be late and 50 percent of the time they'll be early, which means that we should be able to hover around our baseline.

Now let's calculate the rest of the probability scale. If, according to Gauss, 68 percent of my data is within one standard deviation of my mean, that would be 34 percent (half) above the mean and 34 percent below the mean. Thus, the chance of completing my work by the day that falls one standard deviation above my mean date has an 84 percent confidence factor. Using our example, I am 84 percent sure that I can complete the five work packages by day 66.8 or sooner. Conversely, the chance of completing my work by the day that falls one standard deviation below my mean date has a 16 percent confidence

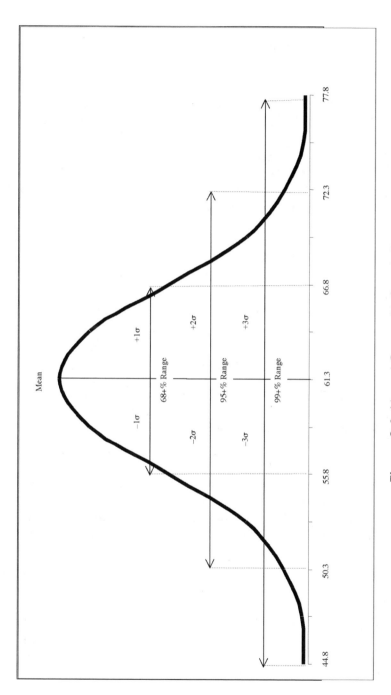

Figure 9-4. Normal Curve with Sample Data

factor. Using our example, I am only 16 percent sure that I can complete the five work packages by day 55.8 or sooner.

For the second standard deviation range, remember that according to Gauss a little more than 95 percent of the data falls in that range. Half of 95 percent would be 47.5 percent; the little bit more takes it to 47.7 percent. Using our example, this would give us a 97.7 percent confidence factor that we can complete the five work packages by day 72.3 or sooner and only a 2.3 percent confidence factor that we can complete the five work packages by day 50.3 or sooner. Figure 9-5 shows the entire scale.

For our third standard deviation range, half of 99 percent is 49.5 percent, but the little bit more takes it to 49.8 percent. Using our example, this gives us a 99.8 percent confidence of completing the five work packages by day 77.8 or sooner and only a 0.2 percent confidence of completing the five work packages by day 44.8 or sooner.

The scariest part of all this analysis is that most of us use only a single-point estimate what we might consider the most likely in our project plans. If we look back at our table of data (Table 9-1), the most likely end date of the project was day 55. According to our probability-of-success scale, we only have a 15 percent confidence that we can complete the five work packages by day 55 or sooner, which is not very confident, and there are only five work packages on the critical path. What do you think happens when you have more work packages on your critical path? That's right, the confidence of completing your plan, based on single-point, most-likely estimates, declines.

Today most project managers plan their entire schedule on one single-point estimate. These projects have a very slim chance of completing exactly on time as displayed on their original plan. However, there's a famous quote in statistics that the "probability never goes to zero" and there's always a slim chance. The prudent project manager would perform at least this minimal amount (PERT) of risk analysis on the project to

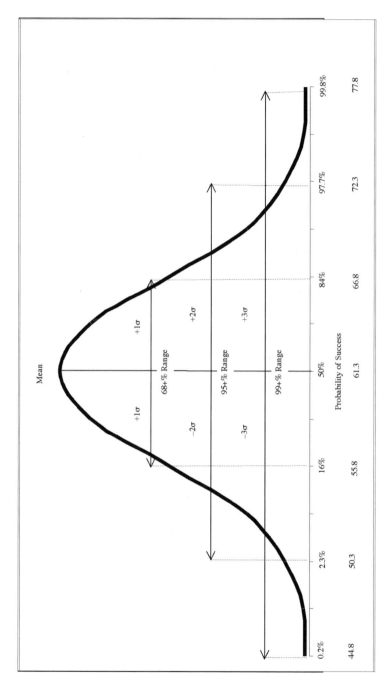

Figure 9-5. Normal Curve with Probability-of-Success Scale

challenge the team to adhere to the most likely schedule, but would also produce a second schedule that has the contingency built in (using the PERT mean) as the date for which the team is really aiming. The really prudent project manager might take the end date up one more standard deviation before giving the customer a delivery date. This would mean that the delivery date to the customer has an 84 percent chance of being met.

But who ever gets the chance to "give" the customer a due date? Most customers wanted the deliverable yesterday. Keep in mind that if the due date is sooner than the date calculated using a statistical analysis (like PERT) as the mean date for finishing all the work, then there is a huge risk to the overall success of the project. That risk needs to be elevated to the appropriate decision-making authority.

Before you elevate this information, though, you might try some of the compression techniques. If the individual work packages each have a calculated mean duration, then the new critical path developed after the network compressions will calculate an end date that theoretically still has a 50 percent chance. This, of course, usually means that additional resources (or more efficient resources) must be assigned to the project.

Depending on the priority of the project, the decision-making authority above you on your project can mitigate this risk by providing the resources needed. The skill level of each additional resource needed, plus the timeframe of when they would be needed, can be determined by identifying those resources that are overutilized in your compressed schedule. If you can obtain a clone of these resources during these timeframes, your schedule has a 50 percent chance of succeeding.

If your decision-making authority does not provide the resources, then they must accept the risk. You can use the normal curve to show the confidence factor for getting all the work completed on time without the proper amount of resources. Using our example, let's say your project sponsor says that the project must be completed by day 50 and that they cannot provide you any other resources; you can show them how the probability of completing the work by that date is 2 percent. Although this is not 0 percent, there is clearly a high risk that the project will not be successful. Moreover, if the project team gets wind of this, they will likely assume defeat, thus sealing the project's fate of not being successful.

Try using PERT in Exercise 9-A.

Exercise 9-A
PERT

Assuming that all the tasks in the chart below are scheduled serially (i.e., they make up one path and it is the critical path of the project), determine the PERT mean, standard deviation, and ranges for the project.

Tasks	Optimistic	Most Likely	Pessimistic	(o+4ml+p)/6	(p−o)/6	([p−o]/6)²
A	8.0	10.0	20.0			
B	14.0	16.0	28.0			
C	3.0	5.0	10.0			
D	12.0	15.0	25.0			
E	3.0	4.0	8.0			
F	20.0	25.0	40.0			
G	6.0	8.0	20.0			
H	4.0	5.0	10.0			
I	15.0	17.0	25.0			
Project			Mean =		$\Sigma([p-o]/6)^2$ =	
					Square Root of $\Sigma([p-o]/6)^2$ =	

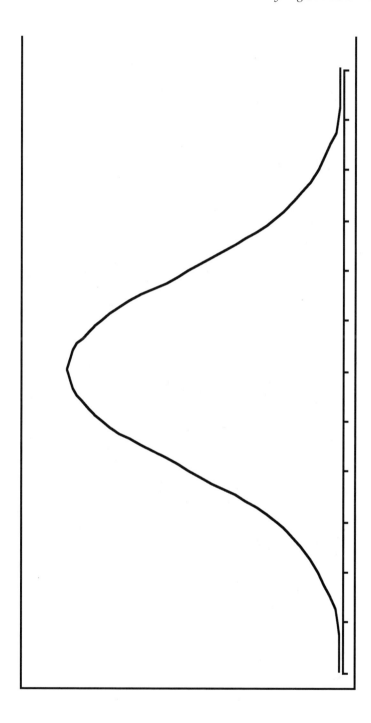

Solution for Exercise 9-A
PERT

MERGE BIAS

Tasks	Optimistic	Most Likely	Pessimistic	(o+4ml+p)/6	(p-o)/6	([p-o]/6)²
A	8.0	10.0	20.0	11.3	2.0	4.0
B	14.0	16.0	28.0	17.7	2.3	5.4
C	3.0	5.0	10.0	5.5	1.2	1.4
D	12.0	15.0	25.0	16.2	2.2	4.7
E	3.0	4.0	8.0	4.5	0.8	0.7
F	20.0	25.0	40.0	26.7	3.3	11.1
G	6.0	8.0	20.0	9.7	2.3	5.4
H	4.0	5.0	10.0	5.7	1.0	1.0
I	15.0	17.0	25.0	18.0	1.7	2.8
Project	105.0		Mean =	115.2	$\Sigma([p-o]/6)^2 =$	36.5
					Square Root of $\Sigma([p-o]/6)^2 =$	6.0

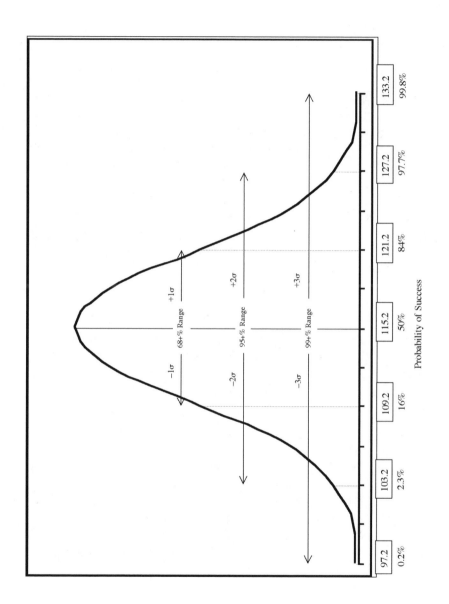

MERGE BIAS

One of the big drawbacks of using PERT to analyze the probability of success of the project schedule is that the analysis method can be performed only on a single path of the project. The summation rule of statistics states that the data being analyzed must be "mutually exclusive," which means that no other data can have an impact on the probability of the event you are analyzing. In the case of schedule risk analysis of just one path, as with PERT, this would mean that no other path of work packages can merge with the critical path that is being used in the analysis.

The inventors of PERT ignored this clause, I assume with the caveat that this would be "good enough for government work .... " They essentially isolated the longest path, gave it the name "the critical path," and performed the analysis as if the work on the other paths, because of the float, could not impact the duration.

Rarely does a well-developed project network schedule consist of only one path of work. The PERT analysis can calculate the individual probability of any number of work package paths; however, at any point where two or more paths merge, a statistical sum occurs. The formula for a statistical sum is:

$$P(A + B) = P(A) * P(B)$$

In other words, if the probability of path A being accomplished by a particular date is 50 percent and the probability of path B being accomplished by that same date is 85 percent (which assumes float equivalent to one standard deviation) and these paths merge on that same expected date, then the probability of both of them reaching that expected date together is 42.5 percent (.5 * .85 = .425). If a third path merges in with a 97 percent chance of accomplishing the work by that date, the merged probability of having all three paths of work accomplished by the date would go even lower, to 41.2 percent (.5 * .85 * .97 = .412).

Commonly known as "merge bias," this is why so many of the risk management experts warn that PERT analysis is not a valid method of schedule risk analysis. However, if you are doing nothing in the area of risk analysis on your network schedule, and are developing your schedule using just one most likely estimate of duration, then you are more or less "shooting yourself in the foot" as it is. Performing a risk analysis on your critical path is a step in the right direction toward developing a plan that has a chance of success. A better method would be to use a simulation.

MONTE CARLO SIMULATION

Another, more complete, method of determining the probability of success of the project schedule is to simulate multiple possible scenarios of the schedule. Monte Carlo simulation was named after Monte Carlo, Monaco, where the primary attractions are casinos containing games of chance. The random behavior in games of chance is similar to how Monte Carlo simulation selects variable values at random to imitate a real-life situation.

This type of simulation is very useful in schedule risk analysis by randomly selecting the duration of the individual work packages in the network schedule. To provide a range for the simulation to randomly select from, the user must provide optimistic, most likely, and pessimistic durations, just like with the PERT analysis, plus an expected distribution. The expected statistical distribution of most project work packages is the "beta distribution," which is similar to the normal curve. Instead of being evenly distributed on either side of the mean, however, the beta distribution is a skewed curve that has more distribution to the right than to the left. This is more true to project tasking because when things go well in a work package the duration will be a bit earlier, whereas when things go wrong, the duration of the work package tends to be impacted to a greater extent.

A number of Monte Carlo simulation software tools are available for project management. They all accomplish the analysis in the same or very similar ways. Once the three estimates—optimistic, most likely, and pessimistic—are entered in the simulation tool and the distribution is selected, the Monte Carlo simulation software performs a user-prescribed number of trials.

For each trial, the software tool randomly selects a duration that falls in the range, using the distribution, for each work package of the network schedule. The software tool then records the calculated end date of the project for each of the trials and provides the tabulated end dates of the range of time that the project can be accomplished with a 5 percent confidence, a 10 percent confidence, etc., stepping up every 5 percent to the date that has a 100 percent confidence. An example of the output of this type of analysis is displayed in Figure 9-6.

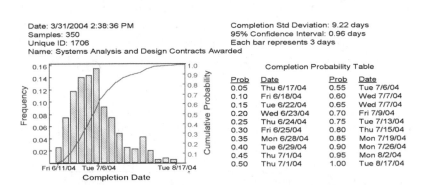

Figure 9-6. Sample Output of Monte Carlo Simulation

As can be seen in Figure 9-6, the outcome dates equate to the confidence level that the analysis of the simulation produced. If the dates with a fairly attainable confidence level (i.e., at least 50 percent) are beyond the expected due date of the project, then the network schedule must be compressed, which usually requires more resources. This must be presented to the sponsor of the project as a major project risk. The sponsor can choose to mitigate the risk by providing the required resources, all of which should have been identified (number, skill level, etc.) by the project manager and team during the compression process. If the project sponsor does not provide the resources to mitigate at least some of the risk, then the project sponsor is choosing to accept the risk. All this should be documented in the project risk register.

As noted, most risk management experts prefer the Monte Carlo method over PERT. The big advantage is that the Monte Carlo simulation of randomly generating duration estimates is performed on all the work packages of the schedule, not just the critical path.

If analyzing the risk and elevating the confidence of completing the work packages of the schedule on time still has not generated a plan that has enough success built in, one other technique can be tried. That technique is to readdress the scope as structured by the deliverable-oriented WBS and possibly determine a usable amount of scope that has a higher chance of success.

10 READDRESSING THE SCOPE TO BALANCE THE TRIPLE CONSTRAINT

Too often project managers go forward at a low confidence level with the notion that "divine intervention" will somehow make everything right. The work tends to swell at the end of the schedule and many items in the scope, usually the wrong scope (like some of the testing work packages), get thrown out at the last minute just to get the deliverable out the door on time. Then when there are "bugs," everyone is surprised.

Balancing the triple constraint is the only way to achieve success.

DE-SCOPING THE PROJECT

If the resources needed to get all the work packages completed by the due date with a certain amount of confidence are just not available, the only other possible recourse is to de-scope the project. This entails prioritizing the deliverables of the WBS so the project can be accomplished with a higher degree of confidence (see Figure 10-1). This goes back to the basic concept of success and how the team members need to feel successful to be successful.

DISPLAYING THE INTEGRATED COST AND SCHEDULE PLAN

Now that we've developed our schedule and rebalanced our scope to the resources that are available to get all the work

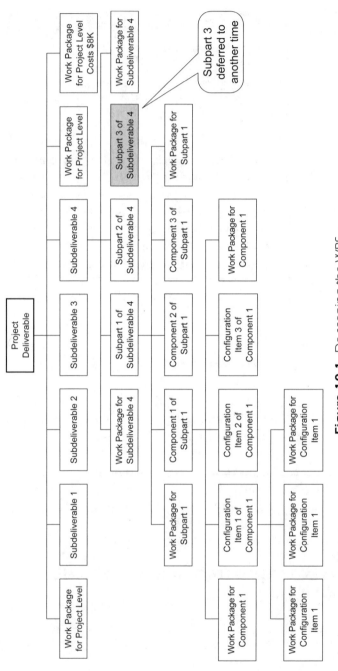

Figure 10-1. De-scoping the WBS

completed in time, we have a balanced triple constraint. To recap, the balanced triple constraint is determining the scope (best solution) for the budget (that their money can buy) in time (for them to use it). But there's one more step before we can move on to the execution of all this work that we so carefully planned. We need to make sure that all our stakeholders are happy with where we are and give their approval for us to move forward.

To get the stakeholders' approval, we must be prepared to show them our plan. One of the best tools for doing this is the Gantt chart.

Henry Gantt, one of the original developers of project management techniques, had no concept of predecessor and successor relationships when he developed his chart back in 1917. The one tool that Gantt gave the project management world is the timescale, using bars to show the progression of work over time. This time-scaled view of the project schedule is still today one of the most useful tools we have for displaying the project schedule. (Although a real Gantt chart does not show the links between work packages, it is a very useful tool nonetheless.)

Too often the project schedule is displayed in too much detail for its audience. If the project schedule is developed well, with all the interdependencies linked together, the detail of the network schedule will be very difficult for someone not already intimately familiar with it to read. Displaying the schedule using the summary Gantt bars of the upper-level deliverables of the WBS and stepping the audience down into the detail one deliverable at a time is a much better technique for displaying the schedule. Figures 10-2 and 10-3 are simple examples of a Gantt chart.

Now that we have displayed our project plan to our stakeholders, who have the authority to make the business decision whether or not the project is still worth pursuing, let's move on to the execution and controlling processes in case we actually get that approval.

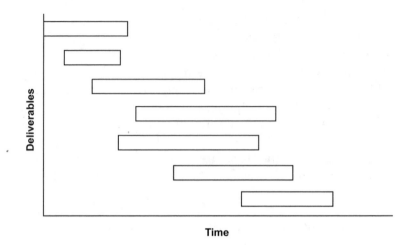

Figure 10-2. Example of Gantt Chart

ID	Task Name	Start	Finish	Duration	Jan 2002				Feb 2002		
					1/6	1/13	1/20	1/27	2/3	2/10	2/17
1	Design Deliverable	1/1/2002	1/7/2002	5d	■						
2	Subdeliverable 1	1/3/2002	2/13/2002	30d	████████████						
3	Subdeliverable 2	1/9/2002	2/5/2002	20d		███████					
4	Subdeliverable 3	1/8/2002	1/28/2002	15d		████					
5	Test Deliverable	2/13/2002	2/15/2002	3d							■

Figure 10-3. Example of Gantt Chart from Project Management
Software Tool

PART 4

THE EXECUTION AND CONTROLLING PROCESS

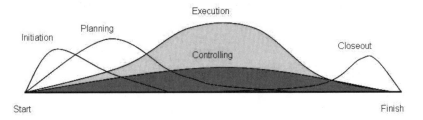

Once the triple constraint for the project, or the current incremental phase of the project, has been balanced, a final decision should be made whether or not to move forward with the project into the execution process. This is commonly referred to as a "go/no go" decision, a "control gate," or a formal integrated baseline review (IBR). All stakeholders should be in agreement, with the right amount of confidence, that the project plan can produce a successful result and that the potential return on the investment of time and costs expended during execution will be acceptable.

If the decision is a "go," then the project (or incremental phase of the project) plan is locked in as a baseline and moves forward to the execution process of the planned work and the controlling process of that execution. By performing cost analysis and applying schedule-adjusting techniques, the project manager can replan all future work to steer back toward the baseline to keep the project's cost and schedule within the predefined control thresholds.

The steps involved in this process are:

1. Establishing and presenting a performance measurement baseline (PMB) of the plan

2. Collecting cost and schedule status data on how well the project is progressing

3. Performing earned value analysis on the status data

4. Redirecting future work back toward the baseline.

11 ESTABLISHING A PERFORMANCE MEASUREMENT BASELINE

The project is now "baselined." This means that:

- The scope of the deliverable is locked in.

- Any new requirements will be considered a change.

- The scheduled start and finish dates of each work package of the project plan are locked in.

- The agreed-upon cost of each work package is allocated as a budget to that work package.

The step of allocating cost to the work package turns each final, agreed-upon estimate of both the effort and the cost to pay for that effort, plus any other expenses, into a budget for that work package for analysis purposes. This budget can be expressed either as effort or as money. The analysis techniques for identifying issues in the execution of the project can be applied the same way on either type of data; however, since the business world is a world of dollars and cents, the common method of performing this analysis, called earned value analysis, is in terms of money.

The baseline is made up of all three components of the triple constraint—scope, budget, and time—and is presented as a graphed line of how the effort or money for the baselined scope is planned to be spent over time.

Figure 11-1 shows a simple schedule of work packages that have their own budgets. Figure 11-2 shows how this information can be displayed on a graph.

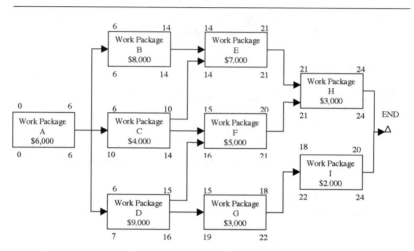

Figure 11-1. Balanced Project Schedule Ready to Be Baselined

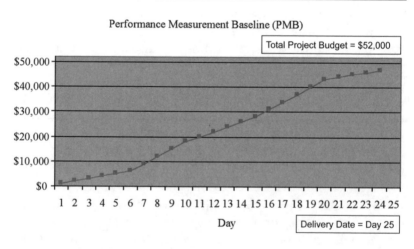

Figure 11-2. Performance Measurement Baseline

BUDGET AT COMPLETION

As can been seen in our example, the performance measurement baseline (PMB) is an accumulation of the individual budgets of each work package over time. The final data point on the PMB chart is the cumulative sum of the budgets of all the work packages in the project. This represents the amount of money or effort we plan to spend at the completion of all the work packages. This data point is called the "budget at completion" (BAC).

The BAC should always be less than the overall budget for the project or incremental phase. The prudent project manager recognizes that problems can occur with any of the work packages, no matter how well risks were identified during the estimation process. Some budget (and also some time) is usually set aside for these unknowns. This is often referred to as "management reserve," because the project manager can only "tap" into this reserve with the approval and full disclosure of the stakeholders.

Management reserve allows for a tolerance control area to be established around the PMB. On many projects the tolerances of this threshold are established at plus or minus 10 percent, which means that approximately 10 percent of the overall budget of the project, or incremental phase, should be set aside as management reserve. For a schedule management reserve, we can use one standard deviation's worth of time (as described in Chapter 9). Earned value analysis provides the indicators that let the project manager know where the project status falls within this threshold.

Note in Figure 11-2 that the budget for the project is $52,000 and the deliverable is due on day 25. This difference of $5,000 from the BAC of $47,000, and one day between day 24 and day 25, is the management reserve.

DISPLAYING THE BASELINE ON THE NETWORK SCHEDULE

Another very important presentation of the baseline that can be used to help the project manager control the execution of the project is the time-scaled network schedule, often referred to as the Gantt view of the schedule. At the moment the baseline is set, a snapshot of the schedule is locked in. This snapshot of the baselined schedule can be presented to the project team so they know what each of them needs to do on the project and when. Each team member can have his or her own individual schedule of the work for which they are responsible. This allows the individual team members, especially the ones who are working on multiple projects, to plan their time effectively.

Most project management software tools will show a gray bar representing the baselined duration of each work package. As the project work packages are being executed, the software tool will show either a blue bar, for a noncritical work package, or a red bar, for a critical work package, showing the schedule changes according to the reality of the progress of the work being accomplished.

Figure 11-3 shows how a project management software tool (in this case MS Project) displays a time-scaled view of both the baselined and the working schedule. Figure 11-4 shows that same time-scaled view where the project has had a late start. Notice how the gray bars have not changed, because they represent the schedule at the time of the baseline. As we will see in Chapter 14, this tool will be very useful in helping the project manager direct the work packages back to the baseline and within control.

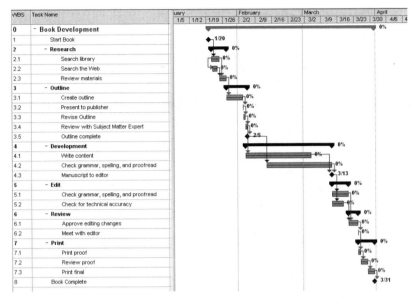

Figure 11-3. Schedule Showing Gray Bars for Baseline

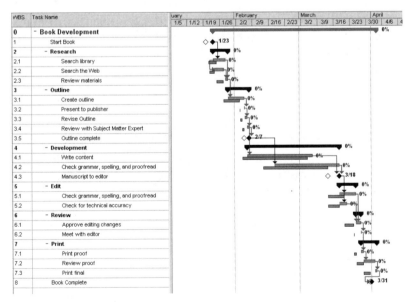

Figure 11-4. Schedule Showing Comparison of Working Bars to Baselined Bars

CHANGING THE BASELINE

One of the primary steps in controlling the cost and schedule during execution of the project, or incremental phase, is to establish a certain discipline on the project baseline (i.e., the baseline never changes unless a formal change management process has taken place). This does not mean that the work packages of the baselined scope cannot be replanned and rescheduled; however, many circumstances that cannot be controlled by any project manager can cause the project to be out of control. If the reality of the cost or schedule status of the project happens to be out of the control area of the baseline, then it is not this reality that is incorrect. The original plan that is represented by the baseline is incorrect and therefore may need to be changed.

Too often this situation of reality not being exactly as we planned is considered a reason for reprimand of the project manager and the project team. The project manager and the team are made to think they did something wrong, when in truth they just might not have been psychic enough when they estimated the parameters of cost and time to know how productivity and availability of resources would change over time during the execution process. Just like the pilot who can continually monitor the productivity of how the fuel of the airplane is being consumed and the availability of the fuel in the tank, he or she cannot always be sure that there will be enough for the flight because circumstances (such as weather) can cause the flight to get out of control. The baseline and the subsequent analysis will allow the project manager to continually monitor the effort and cost consumption of resources; however, that consumption may be quite different from what the project manager estimated prior to the execution process.

All estimates involve risk. While those who approved the plan were no better at predicting the future than were the project manager and the team, by the act of approval they accepted the risk of the estimates and should be held as accountable for their lack of psychic powers.

Both good and bad things happen on all projects. The real technique of controlling the project is to set a threshold on both sides of the baseline that will not only help direct future work, but will also help determine whether or not the baseline serves as a good guidance system. This threshold provides a "control space" that enables the project manager and the project team to "maneuver" in performing various corrective actions on issues, such as performing schedule compression techniques (discussed in Chapter 8). If the cost and schedule status falls outside the threshold and, no matter what the project manager and project team try to do to resolve the issues identified, it is determined that the status will remain outside the threshold, then the change management process should be initiated and a change to the baseline (which is no longer guiding project execution) should be considered.

A number of circumstances can take the project cost or schedule outside the threshold in a flash. Here are just a few:

- Change of requirements

- Loss of a key team member

- Major environmental issue (e.g., fire, flood, hurricane)

- Technological redirection.

A baseline change should not be considered a trivial matter. When any of these situations occur, a change management process should be enacted immediately because the decisions on how to proceed must be made at a higher level of authority than the project manager. These situations are no longer project decisions but are corporate or organizational decisions that should be made at the level of management that approved the project plan when it was baselined.

The other situation that requires the change management process occurs when the project status no longer hovers around the project baseline because the project manager is just not able to control the team's day-to-day actions. The project manager has to make the hard decision of when to go to a higher level of authority, such as his or her manager or project sponsor, for help in setting priorities or providing support. This is a very difficult thing for most project managers to do because no one wants to be the bearer of bad news, but the longer the situation continues, the worse it will get. I can't tell you how often I've seen project teams that really believe that "divine intervention" will prevail and save the situation. The organization that recognizes that the timely identification of bad situations is part of the controlling process and encourages project managers to elevate bad news in a timely manner is the one that will enjoy the benefits of project success.

The change management process should incorporate the following types of activities:

- An agreement by both the customer and the project team on the level of change management control required on the project based on size, importance, complexity, etc.

- A form documenting that the change management process needs to be enacted (e.g., a change request form)

- A group, made up of the project manager and select team members, to investigate the impact of the change on the project scope, budget, and/or schedule

- A governing group of individuals that make the corporate or organizational decisions on how to proceed with the change based on its expected impact

- An agreed amount of budget and time to replan the rest of the project for all approved changes

- A rebaselining of the approved replan.

Without the discipline of a solid baseline—one that can be changed only through a controlled process controlling the cost and schedule of any large, complex project is extremely difficult. The baseline is the guidance system that makes the integrated process of cost and schedule control work.

12 COLLECTING COST AND SCHEDULE PERFORMANCE METRICS

Regularly determining the status of the project is an integral part of the job of managing and controlling its cost and schedule performance. The best project managers recognize that the status report meeting not only gives each team member the opportunity to discuss what they have accomplished or are having difficulties with, but to share in the celebration of accomplishments and to help resolve the difficulties of the other team members. This helps bind the individual team members together as a team by allowing everyone to get involved with the project as a whole.

Status should be reported using the five integrated project management processes:

- *Initiation process.* If any parts of the overall deliverable were not decomposed before this time, the status should report whether or not sufficient information is now available to decompose the deliverable parts to work packages or if they should continue to be deferred as planning packages. Any newly discovered requirements that are identified during the decomposition of the newly identified parts must be analyzed to decide whether or not they still fit in the scope or should be considered out of scope.

  An example of this would be my house (discussed in Chapter 2) and the fact that I did not want to design the details of my kitchen until the frame of the kitchen area was complete. After I could go into the space of my kitchen, I was able to visualize and break down the various possible parts of the kitchen. I could then decide, based on the baselined planning package budget I had set aside for the kitchen, what would go where and what I could do without at this time.

- *Planning process.* Once any new, in-scope requirements are decomposed and their work packages are identified, the work must be planned using all the planning process tools and techniques (introduced in Part 3) and incorporated into the master plan of the project.

- *Execution process.* Any newly planned work packages must be approved and individually baselined within the master plan before work on these work packages can commence. Data on the cost and schedule status of each work package where the work was being executed, both those that have started and those that have been completed, since the last reporting period should be collected.

- *Controlling process.* This process involves analyzing the cost and schedule data collected, identifying issues, and discussing any issues with the team to determine whether corrective action (discussed in Chapters 13 and 14) should take place.

- *Closing process.* The closing process involves capturing lessons learned and determining whether any part of the project deliverable has been completed so that the success of completing that part can be celebrated and properly documented.

The outcome of all these steps should be documented in a regular project status report, noting any action items that are assigned to individual team members. This report should be distributed to each team member for review and acceptance. It can also be used as part of a more formal report to each stakeholder on the status of the project.

PLANNED VALUE

The baseline sets up a guidance system for the project. Just like a flight plan serves as a guidance system for the pilot of an airplane, the baseline aids in directing the project execution to the ultimate goal of accomplishing all the work involved in building the deliverable on time and within budget. Just as for the pilot, the idea is not to be precisely on the baseline, but to be able to hover around the baseline. To do this, we need to know where the baseline is. The data point on the baseline serves as one of the primary earned value analysis data points used in analyzing the schedule status of the project or incremental phase of the project.

The planned value (PV), also known as the budgeted cost of work scheduled (BCWS),[7] is the point on the baseline where the line representing the date that status will be reported intersects the baseline. This line is often referred to as a data date or status date. The PV (BCWS) represents the portion of the budget we expected to spend as of the status date if all work is accomplished exactly as we planned. Figure 12-1 shows how the PV is determined for day 10 using our previous baseline example.

Task A is planned to be completed by day 10, so all of Task A's budget will be in the PV. Task B is planned to be 50 percent complete by day 10, so 50 percent of Task B's budget will be in the PV. Task C is planned to be completed by day 10, so all of Task C's budget will be in the PV. Finally, Task D is planned to have four days of its nine-day duration completed by day 10, so 4/9 of Task D's budget will be in the PV. Table 12-1 shows the PV for this project as of day 10.

---

[7]This change in terms and acronyms occurred early in 2002 under the direction of PMI's College of Performance Management, www. cpm-pmi.org.

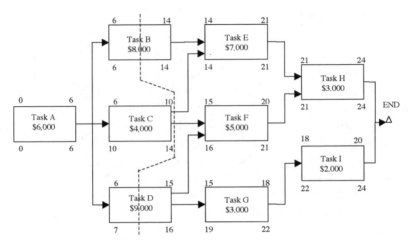

Figure 12-1. Baseline Schedule Showing Status Date

Task	Total Task Budget	Planned Value (PV) As of Day 10
A	$6,000.00	$6,000.00
B	$8,000.00	$4,000.00
C	$4,000.00	$4,000.00
D	$9,000.00	$4,000.00
Project	**$47,000.00**	**$18,000.00**

Table 12-1. Sample Calculation of Planned Value as of Day 10

The project PV can also be displayed using the PMB, as shown in Figure 12-2.

As the project progresses over time, the PV continually increases along the PMB over time. Figure 12-3 displays day 15 on the schedule. As can be seen, Tasks A, B, C, and D are all planned to be completed as of day 15. Task E is planned to have one of its seven days duration completed by day 15. Table 12-2 displays the PV for this example project as of day 15 and Figure 12-4 displays the PV on the PMB.

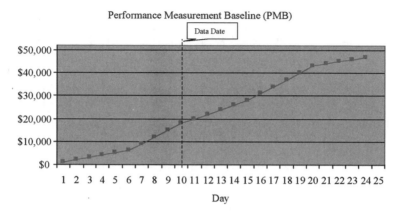

Figure 12-2. PMB with Planned Value as of Day 10 Displayed

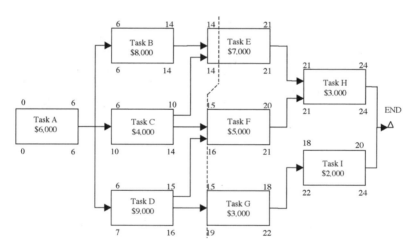

Figure 12-3. Baseline Schedule with Day 15 as Status Date

Task	Total Task Budget	Planned Value (PV) As of Day 10
A	$6,000.00	$6,000.00
B	$8,000.00	$8,000.00
C	$4,000.00	$4,000.00
D	$9,000.00	$9,000.00
E	$7,000.00	$1,000.00
Project	**$47,000.00**	**$28,000.00**

Table 12-2. Sample Calculation of Planned Value as of Day 15

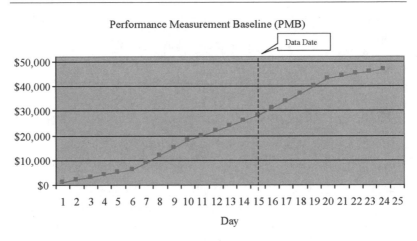

Figure 12-4. Planned Value Displayed Using PMB as of Day 15

ACTUAL COST

The only way that actual progress can be shown on the project schedule is to know whether or not each work package has had an actual start and/or an actual finish. The project management software tools expect the project manager (or someone on the project team) to be entering this information into the tool in order for it to be able to display actual progress on the schedule. To collect the data required to analyze the status of the project's budget, we need additional mechanisms that collect information on actual effort expended and the expenses of each work package. Ideally, this mechanism will also collect estimated remaining effort and expenses needed to complete the work package. The best mechanisms for collecting actual information are timesheets, expense reports, and invoices.

The use of timesheets (see Figure 12-5 for a sample) can be a foreign concept to team members who have never been asked to do this before. It often amazes me how many organizations claim to have control over their projects but have never instilled the discipline of completing timesheets.

Having the actual information of what has been spent on the project so far is critical for cost control. A pilot needs to continually monitor the fuel consumption of the airplane. If they do not have a gauge that provides this information, they can easily run out of fuel while the airplane is still in the air.

The project that runs out of budget before it is complete will have severe consequences also (although certainly not as disastrous). If the project is canceled because it has run out of funds, all the money that has been spent on the project so far has effectively been "poured down the drain."

Collecting actual information about what we do during our workday has a far more positive impact than negative. Importantly, it allows the team members to show the amount of multitasking they are expected to accomplish in an eight-hour day. In today's world, team members are expected to work on a multitude of tasks (some that were in the original schedule and others that were not) all at the same time. We tend to pride ourselves on being able to juggle a number of "balls in the air" at the same time.

The biggest problem with being overwhelmed with work is that it may erode our basic concept of success. We may begin to think we can't do it all, and once that notion of failure seeps into

Figure 12-5. Sample Timesheet

our minds, our productivity declines, perpetuating the failure. Some of us can pull it all together and fight the "failure" feeling, but that fight affects our mental and physical states, which over time will cause many stress-related ailments.

By being able to document the various tasks we perform in our workday, we can show how much we have accomplished and we can use the information to make sure we are not assigned more than we can accomplish. Having a record of what we accomplish can also add to our feeling of success on the project.

Actual cost (AC) (also known as the actual cost of work performed, or ACWP) is the second data point required to be able to perform earned value analysis to help control the cost status of the work packages during the execution process. AC usually involves collecting not only the cost of doing the actual work reported on the timesheets, but also expense reports, invoices, etc., which provide information on the direct costs incurred on the project.

Unfortunately, much of the information collected on the actual costs of the project is often not shared with the project manager. This should not be an excuse, however, for not trying to manage the budget. The earned value data can be analyzed using only the effort hours of the work package. The PV can be collected in terms of effort hours planned and the AC can be collected from the timesheets alone. This still requires that all team members enter their time, by activity or work package, on a timesheet.

EARNED VALUE

The third data point for earned value analysis is the earned value (EV) (also known as the budgeted cost of work performed, or BCWP). EV provides us data, expressed as money or as effort hours, on what has been accomplished on each work package. EV should not consider what was planned to be accomplished on the work package, but instead it should focus on whatever mechanism was identified to measure the work of the work package when the work package was first identified on the WBS. (Remember SMART, introduced in Chapter 4?) Nor should EV consider how much money or effort has been spent on the work package. It is based purely on how much of the deliverable of the work package has truly been completed. This is the only data point that needs to be calculated.

The basic formula for calculating earned value is:

$$EV = \% \text{ Complete}_{\text{work package}} * \text{Budget}_{\text{work package}}$$

The various methods available to calculate EV are nothing more than different methods of determining the percent complete of a work package. The following are some standard methods:

- Actual effort expended on the work package divided by the sum of the actual effort expended on the work package plus the estimated remaining effort needed to complete the work package.

- The physical percent complete of the deliverable the work package is to produce. An example is the number of pages of a book completed and how many more you are expecting to write, or the number of lines of software code written and how many more you estimate will be needed to provide the functionality.

- A further breakdown of the work package into measurable milestones (sometimes called inch-stones) with a predetermined weighting factor on each milestone.

- The 0/100 rule, which does not allow the work package to earn any of the budget until it is 100 percent complete.

- The 20/80 rule, which allows the work package to earn 20 percent of the budget at the time it has an actual start and the other 80 percent at the time it is 100 percent complete.

- The 50/50 rule, which allows the work package to earn 50 percent of the budget at the time it has an actual start and the other 50 percent at the time it is 100 percent complete.

Each of these methods has its advantages and disadvantages; the two that give the most realistic data of EV for a work package are the physical percent complete and the further breakdown of the work package to predetermined measurable milestones. Figure 12-6 demonstrates how earned value is calculated on our example PMB, as of day 10, using the three different "rule" methods. Figure 12-7 shows the calculation of earned value using either (1) a physical percent complete measurement or (2) where the further breakdown of the work packages into milestones with measurement criteria designated to each has been used to determine the percent complete of the work package.

CALCULATING EARNED VALUE FOR LEVEL OF EFFORT

Level of effort work packages are those in which the effort expended does not produce a deliverable, but is needed for general support-type services, such as project management in general or quality audits. We would like to think that any time we expend effort we are producing something, but there are times, especially when working on those oversight tasks that every project requires, that our efforts do not produce tangible deliverables.

The earned value of these types of work packages cannot be calculated because there is no discrete means of measuring the work. Therefore, the EV is set equal to the PV for these types of work packages. The prudent project manager will plan to use

	BCWS	ACWP	Actual Start	Actual Finish	0/100% Rule	20/80% Rule	50/50% Rule
Work Package A	$6,000	$6,500	Yes	Yes	$6,000	$6,000	$6,000
Work Package B	$4,000	$4,200	Yes	No	$0	$1,600	$4,000
Work Package C	$4,000	$3,800	Yes	Yes	$4,000	$4,000	$4,000
Work Package D	$4,000	$2,000	Yes	No	$0	$1,800	$4,500
Project	$18,000	$16,500			$10,000	$13,400	$18,500

Figure 12-6. Calculating Earned Value Using Rule Method

	BCWS	ACWP	Budget	% Complete	BCWP
Work Package A	$6,000	$6,500	$6,000	100%	$6,000
Work Package B	$4,000	$4,200	$8,000	60%	$4,800
Work Package C	$4,000	$3,800	$4,000	100%	$4,000
Work Package D	$4,000	$2,000	$9,000	20%	$1,800
Project	$18,000	$16,500			$16,600

Figure 12-7. Calculating Earned Value Using Measurable Percent Complete

level of effort (LOE) work packages only where discrete deliverables cannot be defined.

DETERMINING PROJECT STATUS DATA USING ONLY EFFORT HOURS

If you do not have information about the costs of the project, you can still determine the PV and the AC, and then calculate the EV. As long as you have the effort budgeted for the work package, you have enough information to use one of the methods for calculating earned value to help control the cost and schedule of the project.

For example, if I have budgeted 80 hours of effort for a work package and the data date falls halfway through that work package, then my PV is 40 hours. If I have a method of measuring the percent complete (any of the rule methods or a true measurement), I can calculate an EV. For example, if I have determined that the work package is 60 percent complete, then the EV calculates to 48 hours earned. If I can determine the actual hours spent on the work package (AC), then I can perform earned value analysis using this data. Even if I can't get the actual hour information, performing the analysis on my schedule, based on the PV and the EV, will yield information that will be very useful in managing the project.

13 PERFORMING EARNED VALUE ANALYSIS

To perform earned value analysis, we need to have collected PV, AC, and EV, plus BAC. The PV, AC, and EV data can be collected and analyzed for both the current-period reporting data and the cumulative data from the beginning of the project. (Figure 13-1 shows the cumulative data graphed on the PMB.)

Earned value analysis falls into two major categories:

- Analysis that measures the performance of the project as of a data date

- Analysis that forecasts what might happen on the project in the future if things do not change.

USING EARNED VALUE ANALYSIS TO ANALYZE COST AND SCHEDULE PERFORMANCE

Three different types of analysis are performed to measure performance:

- Variance

- Performance index

- Project percentage.

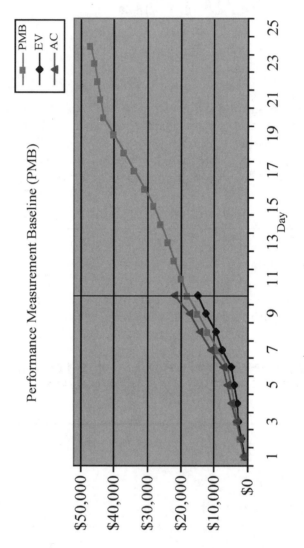

Figure 13-1. Earned Value Data

Variance Analysis

Variances are simple calculations that tell us whether the project is ahead or behind schedule by calculating the schedule variance (SV) and whether the project is showing signs of going over or under budget by calculating the cost variance (CV). The formulas for these two variance indicators are:

$$SV = EV - PV$$

$$CV = EV - AC$$

In both calculations a positive or negative result equates to the status shown in Table 13-1.

Table 13-1. Variance Status Results

	Positive	**Negative**
SV	Ahead of schedule	Behind schedule
CV	Under budget	Over budget

Figure 13-2 shows how the variances can be identified using the PMB.

While variances are nice to know, they are not useful for comparing the performance of one project to another, nor can they be used to isolate issues since they are not relative to the size of what's being analyzed. For example, a -$1,000 CV would have a major impact on a $10,000 project, but only a minor impact on a $100,000 project. To make this analysis technique more meaningful, a further calculation for determining the SV and CV percentages should be used. The formulas for these percentages are:

$$SV\% = \frac{SV}{PV} \qquad CV\% = \frac{CV}{EV}$$

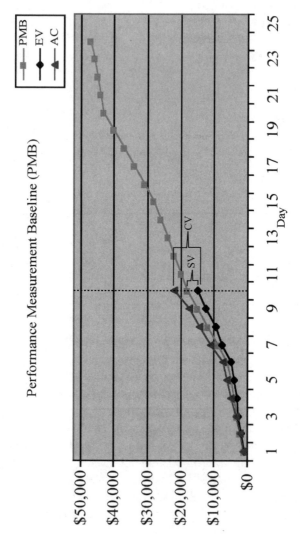

Figure 13-2. *PMB Showing Earned Value Analysis Variances*

Each of these percentages can now be bounded with thresholds, such as plus or minus 10 percent, because they have now made the variance data relative to the size of the project or subpart of the project.

Performance Index Analysis

To calculate a relative-to-size indicator without having to perform two steps, we can use the performance indexes.

The performance indexes calculate performance relative to a unit, such as a dollar or an hour of effort. Here we calculate the schedule performance index (SPI) to determine the performance for every dollar (or whatever unit of currency or effort is being used in the analysis) scheduled to be spent according to the baselined plan. The cost performance index (CPI) tells us the performance for every dollar that has been spent at this time in the project. The formula for these indexes are:

$$SPI = \frac{EV}{PV}$$

$$CPI = \frac{EV}{AC}$$

Let's look at an example:

PV = $45,000

EV = $35,000

AC = $40,000

SV = -$10,000

CV = -$5,000

SPI = 0.78

CPI = 0.86

The SV and the CV, both negative, tell us that the project is behind schedule and over budget. The SPI tells us that for every dollar we planned to spend on this project, we are getting 78 cents worth of performance. The CPI is telling us that for every dollar we have spent so far on this project, we are getting 86 cents worth of performance. If our tolerance is plus or minus 10 percent, we would expect either performance indicator to be between 0.90 and 1.10 to be in control. Since neither is within the thresholds of our control area, we can say our project is out of control in terms of both schedule and cost.

Let's look at a similar example:

PV = $145,000

EV = $135,000

AC = $140,000

SV = -$10,000

CV = -$5,000

SPI = 0.93

CPI = 0.96

The SV and the CV are exactly the same as in the previous example and only tell us that the project is behind schedule and over budget. The SPI tells us that for every dollar we planned to spend on this project, we are getting 93 cents worth of performance. The CPI is telling us that for every dollar we have spent so far on this project, we are getting 96 cents worth of performance. With a tolerance of plus or minus 10 percent, both are within the thresholds of our control area, so we can say this project is in control in terms of both schedule and cost.

Thus, the performance indicators are relative to the size of the project and produce much more useful information than the variances alone. Relevance-to-size indicators also lend themselves very well to being charted individually over time. Figure 13-3 shows the SPI, both current and cumulative, and Figure 13-4 shows the same for the CPI.

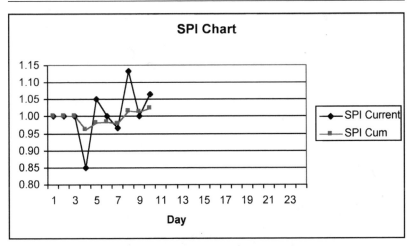

Figure 13-3. SPI Chart

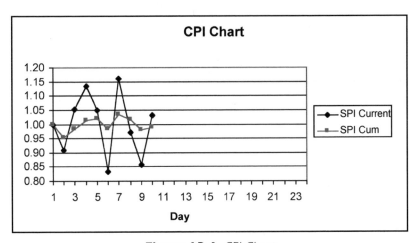

Figure 13-4. CPI Chart

Today many of us use what is sometimes called a "stoplight" chart to show the status of the project. The color "green" is used to show that the status of the project is excellent; the color "yellow" is used to show that the project has some issues and caution should be exercised; and the color "red" shows that the project status is unsatisfactory. Too often these colors are subjectively determined by the project manager based on only a "gut feeling."

The SPI and the CPI allow an objective tolerance range to be established for these colors; for example, an indicator of ≥ .95 and ≤ 1.05 is green, ≥ .90 and < .95 or > 1.05 and ≤ 1.10 is yellow, and < .90 or > 1.10 is red. Figures 13-5 and 13-6 show these color bands on the SPI and CPI charts.

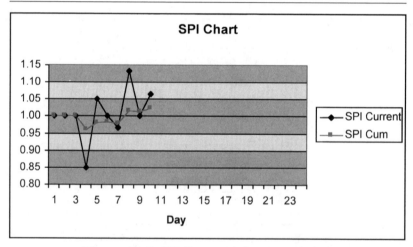

Figure 13-5. SPI Chart with Stoplight Colors

In general, projects do not get "blown over by hurricanes or tornadoes." Instead, they get "eaten by termites." In other words, small issues that occur at the work package level tend to compound if they are not identified and dealt with in time.

This is where our detailed deliverable-oriented work breakdown structure (WBS), developed during the project initiation

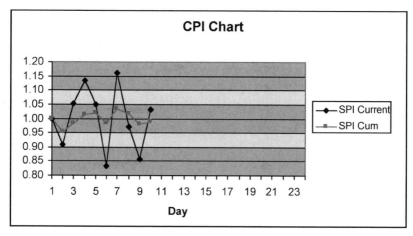

Figure 13-6. CPI Chart with Stoplight Colors

process, becomes so useful during the controlling process. A WBS that is not decomposed to a level where all the real work has been identified will not indicate that there are "termites" until a "wall falls down." A WBS that doesn't have the right parent-child breakdown based on the deliverable can do nothing more than lump problems into what some call "rework."

A deliverable-oriented parent-child WBS can keep all the work involved in completing any part of the project together with that part. It can isolate any issues to an individual part so that the right decisions, based on the importance of the part and the impact to the other parts of the project, can be made.

As an example, let's use a low-level deliverable several levels down in the WBS. This can be any type of deliverable, but for this example, let's say it is a software function that is being developed. The work packages are to design how this function is to be coded, to code the function, and then to unit-test the function. The module that this function is a child of has its own design for how the various functional parts of the module must work together during an integration test of the module.

Let's say that a team member, Tom, has been assigned to complete these three work packages and deliver this function to another, more experienced team member, Mary, who is in charge of the development of the software module in which the function is being integrated. Tom has estimated three days for the design, four days for the code, and two days for the unit test. If Tom's labor rate for this project is $125 per hour, this equates to $3,000 for design, $4,000 for code, and $2,000 for unit test. Figure 13-7 shows the baselined schedule for this scenario.

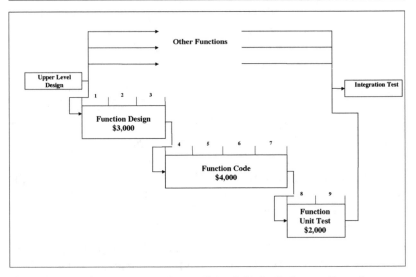

Figure 13-7. Example Status Schedule for Software Function Development

Tom will be expected to report status of his function to Mary. He should provide the status for work that has been accomplished and work that still needs to be accomplished on each open work package.

Figure 13-8 shows that the status date falls after the second day of design. The PV as of that date is $2,000 (which was planned to be spent according to the baselined schedule and where the data date lies). From the company's activity-based cost accounting system, Tom's AC has been reported as $2,375. Tom reports to Mary that he has completed the design of this function and is ready to start coding it. In earned value terms, Tom has earned (EV) $3,000, since the task is 100 percent complete.

The CV (EV – AC) for Tom's function is +$625 ($3,000 - $2,375), which, being positive, means that he is under budget, and the SV (EV – PV) is +$1,000 ($3,000 - $2,000), which, being positive, means that he is ahead of schedule.

Tom's CPI (EV/AC) is 1.26 ($3,000/$2,375) and his SPI (EV/PV) is 1.50 ($3,000/$2,000). Both are outside a 10 percent tolerance in a positive direction, which concerns Mary but can be easily explained.

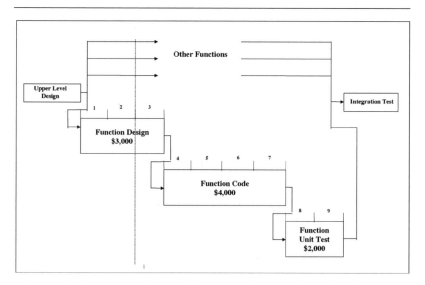

Figure 13-8. Example Status Schedule with Data Date Two Days into Function Design

Time marches on. As shown in Figure 13-9, the new status date is after the fifth day into Tom's function baseline or after the second day of Tom's code work package.

His PV as of today is $5,000. Let's say his AC is reported at $5,250. Tom reports that he has been working on the code for three days (remember he finished the design a day early and therefore started on the code a day earlier than planned) and he thinks he can wrap it up by the end of tomorrow. He has earned (EV), based on being 100 percent complete with design and 75 percent complete with coding (he has completed three days and still believes it is a four-day work package) of $6,000.

Tom's CV is +$750 ($6,000 - $5,250), which means that he is still under budget, and his SV is +$1,000 ($6,000 - $5,000), which means he is still ahead of schedule.

His CPI is 1.14 ($6,000/$5,250) and his SPI is 1.20 ($6,000/$5,000). Both are still out of tolerance in the positive direction but are coming back toward the baseline.

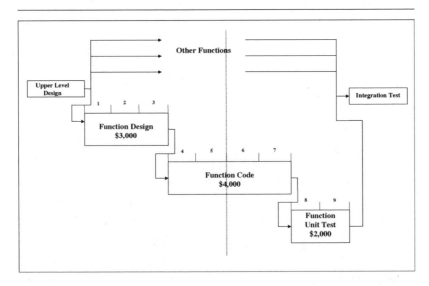

Figure 13-9. Example Status Schedule with Data Date Two Days into Function Code

Again, time marches on. As seen in Figure 13-10, it is now after the eighth day of Tom's deliverable baseline or after the first day of his baselined unit test work package. The PV for Tom's deliverable, as of today, is $8,000. Let's say the AC is reported as $8,075. Mary finds Tom in the test room "sweating bullets." Tom cannot get the code to perform the function it was designed to do.

How much has Tom earned? He definitely has earned nothing for the test because he will have to rerun the tests from the beginning once he fixes the problem. We could say that he has lost value for his design task, because he's back redesigning, and also for his code task, because he'll probably have to write some new code. A relative determination on Tom's earned value in his design task and his code task can be made based on how much additional time he now needs to fix the design and code. In both tasks, however, he has "lost" value, not earned it.

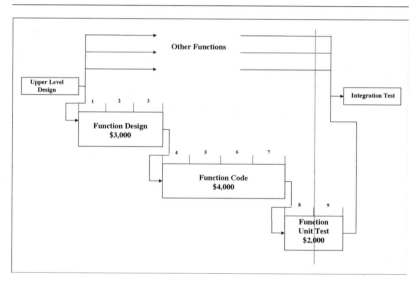

Figure 13-10. Example Status Schedule with Data Date One Day into Function Unit Test

This is the beauty of earned value analysis and the deliverable-oriented WBS. The PV always increases, because it is based on the data date moving along, with time, on the PMB. The AC always increases since we pay for time spent trying to accomplish the work, whether that work is completed or not. The EV, though, can increase as well as decrease: You can earn it and you can lose it, and you will never earn it all until you actually finish the deliverable you've been assigned.

Let's say, for this example, that Tom thinks that most of his design is good. Mary can say that his design work package is 75 percent complete and has earned $2,250 (75%*$3,000). If he also thinks that most of his code is good, then Mary can say that his code task is then 80 percent complete and he has earned $3,200 for that work package. He has earned nothing for test, so his deliverable's EV is $5,450. His CV is -$2,625, his SV is -$2,550, his CPI is 0.67, and his SPI is 0.68—indicating that he's in trouble.

Tom's function, a "termite," is now caught. But all is not gloom and doom; Tom still has a day on the original schedule to fix and test his deliverable without any repercussions. That equates to 24 hours or, if this day happens to be a Friday, 72 hours to fix and test the problem with the code. If he can complete the unit test by the end of day nine, the PV will be $9,000, the AC will probably be around $9,000 (since we will not be expecting Tom to charge us for any of his overtime), and the EV will be $9,000—and Tom should be recognized in some fashion for coming through.

If Tom cannot complete the unit test, Mary will need to address the impact on the integration test work package. Can she take any actions that will enable the integration test to start on time? Her decision is very much based on the importance of Tom's function to the other functions of the module. If Tom's function is a driving function of the module, then maybe she can get Tom some help to correct the problem in the time allotted or as quickly as possible ("crashing"). If it is not a driving function, she can make the decision to change the link between Tom's function deliverable and her integration test work package from finish-to-start to finish-to-finish, with enough lag to allow Tom's function to be fully tested. This allows the integration test of the module to proceed with any of the other functional deliverables that are ready ("fast tracking").

Mary would then plan to bring Tom's deliverable into the test when Tom estimates it will be completed (see Figure 13-11). If Tom's deliverable can be integrated and tested by the time Mary's module is scheduled to be complete, everything is right back on schedule and Mary and her team's accomplishments should be recognized.

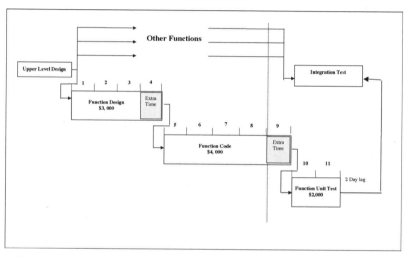

Figure 13-11. *Example Status Schedule with Two-Day Lead Added between Function Unit Test and Integration Test*

The beauty of all of this is that Tom knows the situation. And Tom knows that you, the project manager over Mary, only need to look down the WBS and see that he has a situation on his hands. In other words, Tom knows that you know that Tom knows that you know that he knows .... That's control.

If the WBS is constructed in a deliverable orientation with project management responsibility assigned to each lower-level deliverable, then when the project's CPI or SPI at the top level slips just slightly, it will be obvious which lower-level deliverable is causing the slip. In Figure 13-12, the project-level indicators are certainly in control (SPI = 0.99 and CPI = 0.98), but the third subsystem of the first subdeliverable is showing indicators that are outside a plus or minus 10 percent threshold; the team responsible for that deliverable should be scrambling to bring it back into control or preparing for some serious explaining. They know it and they know you know it.

Because you can see that the third subsystem of the second subdeliverable is way ahead of schedule, you can start identifying resources that might be able to help to complete the work of the first subdeliverable faster. Orchestrating resources in this manner is an essential technique of managing the schedule, and ultimately the costs, of any project.

Project Percentage Analysis

The third category of performance measurement that can be made using earned value analysis is determining the percent planned, versus the percent complete, versus the percent spent on the project as a whole. This is done using the following formulas:

$$\text{Percent Planned} = \frac{PV}{BAC}$$

$$\text{Percent Complete} = \frac{EV}{BAC}$$

$$\text{Percent Spent} = \frac{AC}{BAC}$$

These indicators are normally reported to management when the status of the project is presented.

Let's use the following example:

PV = $45,000

EV = $35,000

	BAC	BCWS	ACWP	BCWP	SV	SPI	CV	CPI
Project deliverable design	$ 43,570	$ 43,570	$ 42,963	$ 43,570	$ 0	1.00	$ 607	1.01
SD1 design	$ 15,000	$ 15,000	$ 15,450	$ 15,000	$ 0	1.00	$ (450)	0.97
SD1-SS1-design	$ 7,560	$ 7,560	$ 7,600	$ 7,560	$ 0	1.00	$ (40)	0.99
SD1-SS1-component 1	$ 123,750	$ 61,875	$ 63,120	$ 61,875	$ 0	1.00	$ (1,245)	0.98
SD1-SS1-component 2	$ 65,450	$ 32,725	$ 31,855	$ 32,725	$ 0	1.00	$ 870	1.03
SD1-SS1-component 3	$ 42,500	$ 21,250	$ 20,750	$ 21,250	$ 0	1.00	$ 500	1.02
SD1-SS1-integration test	$ 14,560	$ 0	$ 0	$ 0	$ 0		$ 0	
SD1-SS2-design	$ 5,600	$ 5,600	$ 5,500	$ 5,600	$ 0	1.00	$ 100	1.02
SD1-SS2-component 1	$ 75,000	$ 37,500	$ 36,700	$ 36,000	$ (1,500)	0.96	$ (700)	0.98
SD1-SS2-component 2	$ 29,560	$ 14,780	$ 15,250	$ 15,000	$ 220	1.01	$ (250)	0.98
SD1-SS2-component 3	$ 78,960	$ 39,480	$ 41,000	$ 42,000	$ 2,520	1.06	$ 1,000	1.02
SD1-SS2-integration test	$ 9,500	$ 0	$ 0	$ 0	$ 0		$ 0	
SD1-SS3-design	$ 8,560	$ 8,560	$ 8,400	$ 8,560	$ 0	1.00	$ 160	1.02
SD1-SS3-component 1	$ 56,000	$ 28,000	$ 27,350	$ 22,400	$ (5,600)	0.80	$ (4,950)	0.82
SD1-SS3-component 2	$ 76,500	$ 38,250	$ 30,450	$ 25,245	$ (13,005)	0.66	$ (5,205)	0.83
SD1-SS3-component 3	$ 44,340	$ 22,170	$ 16,250	$ 14,632	$ (7,538)	0.66	$ (1,618)	0.90
SD1-SS3-integration test	$ 14,750	$ 0	$ 0	$ 0	$ 0		$ 0	
SD1 integration test	$ 25,000	$ 0	$ 0	$ 0	$ 0		$ 0	
SD2 design	$ 16,750	$ 16,750	$ 16,856	$ 16,750	$ 0	1.00	$ (106)	0.99
SD2-SS1-design	$ 4,400	$ 4,400	$ 4,000	$ 4,400	$ 0	1.00	$ 400	1.10
SD2-SS1-component 1	$ 236,000	$ 59,000	$ 75,875	$ 66,080	$ 7,080	1.12	$ (9,795)	0.87
SD2-SS1-component 2	$ 54,280	$ 13,570	$ 15,750	$ 14,656	$ 1,086	1.08	$ (1,094)	0.93
SD2-SS1-component 3	$ 63,200	$ 15,800	$ 16,000	$ 15,800	$ 0	1.00	$ (200)	0.99
SD2-SS1-integration test	$ 8,200	$ 0	$ 0	$ 0	$ 0		$ 0	
SD2-SS2-design	$ 8,500	$ 8,500	$ 7,695	$ 8,500	$ 0	1.00	$ 805	1.10
SD2-SS2-component 1	$ 146,000	$ 36,500	$ 37,000	$ 36,500	$ 0	1.00	$ (500)	0.99
SD2-SS2-component 2	$ 45,000	$ 11,250	$ 12,125	$ 11,250	$ 0	1.00	$ (875)	0.93
SD2-SS2-component 3	$ 255,000	$ 63,750	$ 63,500	$ 63,750	$ 0	1.00	$ 250	1.00
SD2-SS2-integration test	$ 15,500	$ 0	$ 0	$ 0	$ 0		$ 0	
SD2-SS3-design	$ 5,000	$ 5,000	$ 5,200	$ 5,000	$ 0	1.00	$ (200)	0.96
SD2-SS3-component 1	$ 56,400	$ 5,640	$ 6,995	$ 7,050	$ 1,410	1.25	$ 55	1.01
SD2-SS3-component 2	$ 210,830	$ 21,083	$ 26,675	$ 26,354	$ 5,271	1.25	$ (321)	0.99
SD2-SS3-component 3	$ 22,000	$ 2,200	$ 2,325	$ 2,200	$ 0	1.00	$ (125)	0.95
SD2-SS3-integration test	$ 12,480	$ 0	$ 0	$ 0	$ 0		$ 0	
SD2 integration test	$ 47,500	$ 0	$ 0	$ 0	$ 0		$ 0	
Project deliverable system/acceptance test	$ 56,800	$ 0	$ 0	$ 0	$ 0		$ 0	

Figure 13-12. Earned Value Analysis of WBS Percent Complete

AC = $40,000

SV = -$10,000

CV = -$5,000

SPI = 0.78

CPI = 0.86

Let's say that the BAC of this example is $100,000. The resulting percentages would be:

Percent Planned = $45,000/$100,000 = 45%

Percent Complete = $35,000/$100,000 = 35%

Percent Spent = $40,000/$100,000 = 40%

We could then report that we planned to be 45 percent complete with the project, but we are only 35 percent complete. Also, we spent 40 percent of the budget to get to our 35 percent complete point. Another way of looking at the budget is that we have 65 percent of the work still to complete with only 60 percent of the budget remaining.

USING EARNED VALUE ANALYSIS TO FORECAST FUTURE COST ISSUES

Just like the pilot of a plane, a project manager must monitor the resources needed for the future of the project. The second category of earned value analysis formulas helps us do just that. The four subcategories of using EV analysis to forecast future cost issues are:

- Projecting how much money or effort the project might require if the performance trend remains the same

- Using what has been spent so far to calculate how much money or effort might be needed to complete the project

- Calculating the variance at the completion of the project if this forecast holds true

- Determining the performance needed to bring the project back on track.

HOW MUCH COULD THE ENTIRE PROJECT COST?

The earned value analysis formula for predicting what the total project costs could be if things do not change is called the estimate at completion (EAC). Methods for estimating and calculating this factor range from taking your best guess to using the most pessimistic combination of the performance indicators. The following are two formulas (of a multitude available) for various analytical situations:

- A simple way: $EAC = \dfrac{BAC}{CPI}$

- A more complex way: $EAC = AC + \dfrac{BAC - EV}{CPI * SPI}$

Using our sample data:

PV = $45,000

EV = $35,000

AC = $40,000

SV = -$10,000

CV = -$5,000

SPI = 0.78

CPI = 0.86

BAC = $100,000

Our EAC using both formulas would be:

EAC_{Simple} = $100,000/0.86 = $116,279

$EAC_{Complex}$ = $40,000 + ($100,000 - $35,000)/0.86 * 0.78

= $40,000 + $65,000/0.67

= $40,000 + $97,015

= $137,015

The complex method is much more pessimistic than the simple method in this example. This is largely because the complex method takes into consideration the performance of the schedule, which in this case was 0.78, and the fact the team may perceive the low performance of the schedule as "failure," which could slow down their performance even more.

Keep in mind that all this forecasting analysis is still trying to predict the future and should always be qualified with the caveat "if things do not change."

Project managers are often reluctant to use either of these two formulas. When the project is in its latter stages, however, and they are shown that using the formulas would have provided them better information earlier, they realize that they might have been able to do something about their problems before they became serious issues.

HOW MUCH WILL BE NEEDED TO COMPLETE THE PROJECT?

A calculation of how much money or effort might be needed to complete the project, if things do not change, is known as the estimate to complete (ETC):

$$ETC = EAC - AC$$

For our sample using the complex EAC:

$$ETC = \$137{,}015 - \$40{,}000 = \$97{,}015$$

In this example we might need almost as much as our original budget to complete the rest of the work of the project.

ARE WE OVER OR UNDER THE BUDGET AT COMPLETION?

Another simple calculation that will tell us if the project is likely to overrun or underrun the budget if things do not change is the variance at completion (VAC):

$$VAC = BAC - EAC$$

With our sample data:

$$VAC = \$100,000 - \$137,015 = -\$37,015$$

Again, if the VAC is negative, the project could go over budget. If the project is in control (i.e., within the tolerance threshold), then the VAC will be within the management reserve.

WHAT PERFORMANCE DO WE NEED TO GET BACK ON TRACK?

The to-complete-performance-index (TCPI) is calculated by taking the money, or effort hours, remaining and dividing it by the work remaining:

$$TCPI = \frac{BAC - EV}{BAC - AC}$$

For our sample data:

$$TCPI = (\$100,000 - \$40,000)/(\$100,000 - \$35,000)$$

$$= \$65,000/\$60,000 = 1.08$$

This represents the amount of performance needed, from the data date forward, to complete the project for the budget that was baselined. This indicator is often mistakenly used to justify the amount of unpaid overtime each resource must accept for the rest of the project. The prudent project manager knows that unpaid overtime is not a way to increase productivity. As a rule of thumb, if this indicator is 20 percent above the CPI (which it is in our example case), then a change to the baseline, via the change management process, should be considered.

Now that we've seen all the formulas, let's try the following two exercises.

Exercise 13-A
EARNED VALUE ANALYSIS

You are a project manager, in Washington, D.C., in charge of installing security systems in airports.

Your baselined plan is as follows:

Week 1, you send a team to install 10 systems at Baltimore/ Washington International Airport (BWI). The budget for this work package is $1,500/system.

Week 2, the same team will install 10 systems at Philadelphia International Airport (PHI). The budget for this work package is $2,200/system.

Week 3, the same team will install 10 systems at New York's LaGuardia Airport. The budget for this work package is $3,000/ system.

Today is one-and-a-half weeks into this installation project. Your team has installed 13 systems (10 at BWI and 3 at PHI). The costs collected so far equal $24,500.

Calculate:

CV (EV – AC) _____

SV (EV – PV) _____

CPI (EV/AC)_____

SPI (EV/PV) _____

EAC (BAC/CPI)_____

ETC (EAC – AC)_____

VAC (BAC – EAC) _____

Percent Planned (PV/BAC) _____

Percent Complete (EV/BAC) _____

Percent Spent (AC/BAC) _____

Solution for Exercise 13-A
EARNED VALUE ANALYSIS

CV	-$2,900
SV	-$4,400
CPI	.88
SPI	.83
EAC	$76,136
ETC	$51,636
VAC	-$9,136
Percent Planned	39%
Percent Complete	32%
Percent Spent	37%

Exercise 13-B
ANOTHER EARNED VALUE ANALYSIS

Complete the table and analysis by determining whether the task is behind or ahead of schedule, over or under budget, and within a schedule or cost tolerance of plus or minus 10 percent.

Task	PV	AC	EV	SV	SPI	CV	CPI	Analysis of Schedule	Analysis of Cost
A	$8,555	$8,750	$7,750						
B	$4,100	$4,250	$3,975						
C	$5,560	$5,600	$5,675						
D	$6,674	$6,775	$7,500						
E	$10,550	$11,000	$10,450						
F	$25,000	$25,785	$24,750						
G	$2,575	$3,000	$2,275						
H	$16,755	$17,000	$16,500						

Project	PV	AC	EV	SV	SPI	CV	CPI	BAC	EAC
								$1,000,000	

Solution for Exercise 13-B
ANOTHER EARNED VALUE ANALYSIS

Task	PV	AC	EV	SV	SPI	Analysis of Schedule	CV	CPI	Analysis of Cost
A	$8,555	$8,750	$7,750	-$805	0.91	Behind schedule, out of tolerance	-$1,000	0.89	Over budget, out of tolerance
B	$4,100	$4,250	$3,975	-$125	0.97	Behind schedule, in tolerance	-$275	0.94	Over budget, in tolerance
C	$5,560	$5,600	$5,675	$115	1.02	Ahead of schedule, in tolerance	$75	1.01	Under budget, out of tolerance
D	$6,674	$6,775	$7,500	$825	1.12	Ahead of schedule, out of tolerance	$725	1.11	Under budget, in tolerance
E	$10,550	$11,000	$10,450	-$100	0.99	Behind schedule, in tolerance	-$550	0.95	Over budget, in tolerance
F	$25,000	$25,785	$24,750	-$250	0.99	Behind schedule, in tolerance	-$1,035	0.96	Over budget, out of tolerance
G	$2,575	$3,000	$2,275	-$300	0.88	Behind schedule, out of tolerance	-$725	0.76	Over budget, out of tolerance
H	$16,755	$17,000	$16,500	-$255	0.98	Behind schedule, in tolerance	-$500	0.97	Over budget, in tolerance

Project	PV	AC	EV	SV	SPI	CV	CPI	BAC	EAC
	$79,770	$82,160	$78,875	-$895	0.99	-$3,285	0.96	$1,000,000	$1,041,667

14 STEERING FUTURE PERFORMANCE BACK TOWARD THE BASELINE

Earned value analysis not only helps the project manager identify issues, but it can also provide the cost and schedule status information that our stakeholders are seeking when they want to know how the project is going. If we present information that identifies the issues of the project without presenting how we plan to resolve each issue, however, many questions will arise.

The project manager can do little about the cost status of the project actual cost (AC)—also known as "sunk" cost. The only technique available to the project manager to control future costs is to make sure that resources are used as efficiently as possible on the remaining work of the project. If the earned value analysis indicates that project costs are truly out of control, then just like a pilot who has to land to pick up more fuel, the project manager requires either additional budget or a reduction in scope to maintain a successful cost-control posture.

To promote efficient use of the resources for the remaining work of the project, the project manager must do whatever he or she can to promote the success of the remaining work. The project schedule should always be considered a "living" plan: Just because the plan is baselined does not mean that it cannot be adjusted as needed to direct all future work back toward the baseline. We must constantly be aware that project management is not being precisely on the baseline, but it is constantly making the appropriate proactive adjustments to the schedule that are needed to stay in the control area of the baseline.

Having a project management tool (see Figure 14-1) that displays the impact that any slip in the work packages of our baselined plan will have on all future work is a big help for any project. These software tools provide a lot of information, but their most important task is to recalculate that forward and backward pass every time something does not go exactly as planned. The tools perform this recalculation in an instant and then provide two of the most important pieces of information for any project: the total float (can the work package slip?) and the free float (if it slips, will there be an impact on anything else?).

Knowing that a work package has free float (e.g., Work Package 4.1 - Write content) allows the project manager not to have to worry about a delay of that work package, as long as the delay does not go beyond the amount of float that is free (in this case 4.13 days). Knowing that a work package has total float but does not have free float allows the project manager to be proactive in identifying those work packages that will be impacted if this work package slips. The project manager should then analyze the impact and determine what, if anything, should be done, such as calling the resources assigned to an impacted work package and alerting them of the slip beforehand, determining if the impacted work packages can be replanned to be done in parallel instead of in series, or getting some help for the work package that has an issue so it can be completed on time.

If the work package that has an issue does not have float, it is on the critical path, which means that it can impact the entire project's end date and cause the project to be late. All succeeding work packages would then have negative float, as is the case with all but one of the work packages of our example in Figure 14-1. This plan shows that, unless an adjustment is made to the future work packages of the schedule, the project will be late. The project manager would then need to use a schedule compression technique (discussed in Chapter 8) to replan the future work back toward the baseline.

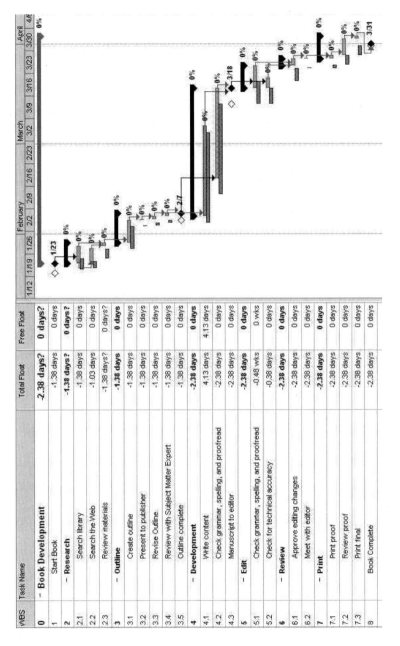

WBS	Task Name	Total Float	Free Float
0	**– Book Development**	**-2.38 days?**	**0 days?**
1	Start Book	-1.38 days	0 days
2	**– Research**	**-1.38 days?**	**0 days?**
2.1	Search library	-1.38 days	0 days
2.2	Search the Web	-1.03 days	0 days
2.3	Review materials	-1.38 days?	0 days?
3	**– Outline**	**-1.38 days**	**0 days**
3.1	Create outline	-1.38 days	0 days
3.2	Present to publisher	-1.38 days	0 days
3.3	Revise Outline	-1.38 days	0 days
3.4	Review with Subject Matter Expert	-1.38 days	0 days
3.5	Outline complete	-1.38 days	0 days
4	**– Development**	**-2.38 days**	**0 days**
4.1	Write content	4.13 days	4.13 days
4.2	Check grammar, spelling, and proofread	-2.38 days	0 days
4.3	Manuscript to editor	-2.38 days	0 days
5	**– Edit**	**-2.38 days**	**0 days**
5.1	Check grammar, spelling, and proofread	-0.48 wks	0 wks
5.2	Check for technical accuracy	-0.38 days	0 days
6	**– Review**	**-2.38 days**	**0 days**
6.1	Approve editing changes	-2.38 days	0 days
6.2	Meet with editor	-2.38 days	0 days
7	**– Print**	**-2.38 days**	**0 days**
7.1	Print proof	-2.38 days	0 days
7.2	Review proof	-2.38 days	0 days
7.3	Print final	-2.38 days	0 days
8	Book Complete	-2.38 days	0 days

Figure 14-1. Time-Scaled Network Diagram Showing Impact of Late Start

By providing additional resources, we can crash work package 4.2 – Check grammar, spelling, and proofread. This would allow this work package to be completed more quickly and the entire schedule would be back to the baseline (shown in Figure 14-2).

For cost and schedule control, the project manager should always be looking to the future and steering the project toward success.

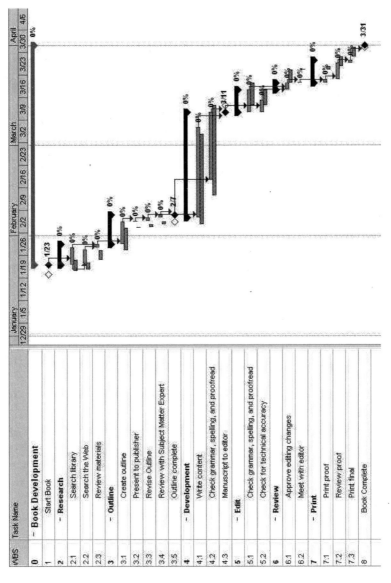

Figure 14-2. Time-Scaled Network Diagram after Compression

PART 5 THE CLOSEOUT PROCESS

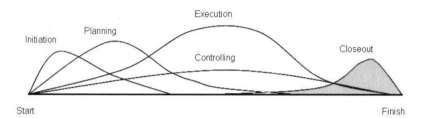

The closeout process is often ignored. Usually when we are toward the end of any project we have grown quite tired of the process and are anxious to move on to another project. However, how well a project is closed out can make or break its real success.

The closeout process involves:

- Analyzing the integrated cost and schedule performance of a completed deliverable

- Using the current project analysis to continuously improve all future project cost and schedule control.

15 ANALYZING THE COST AND SCHEDULE METRICS OF DELIVERABLES

As discussed in Chapter 12, the closeout process should not be held until the end of the project, but should be addressed at each status meeting where a deliverable no matter how far down the WBS it resides has been identified as being complete. As deliverables are completed we should start capturing information that will help determine if the customer will still get their money's worth and if they will get at least a usable portion of the entire project deliverable in time to use it.

To determine whether a deliverable is complete, we must analyze the deliverable based on its usability at the next level up the WBS. If the deliverable is at the lower levels of the WBS, the question to analyze is whether it is ready to be delivered to the next level up and whether it can be used in the integration of a higher-level deliverable. This is an iterative step of building the overall deliverable that the customer will be able to use. As we go through this process, we can determine whether or not each lower-level deliverable truly fulfills the customer's need.

During this process we can start formulating questions that might be used in a customer or user survey to help determine overall customer satisfaction and ultimately be used to measure whether or not we will realize a return on the investment that was made to produce the deliverable. Often a deliverable that overran the budget was still deemed a success because the user loved it and the return was much greater than the investment made.

The use of the deliverable is the ultimate measure of the project's success, regardless of the cost incurred and schedule delays. A project deliverable that is not used is a waste of time and money no matter how well the costs and schedule of producing it were controlled.

At each status meeting we should capture information on the actual effort, the actual cost of that effort, and other expenses required to complete the effort, plus the actual duration of time it took to build each deliverable. The comparison of these actual metrics to the estimates made during the initiation and planning processes, plus the issues encountered that might have impacted these differences, are invaluable pieces of information to be used in the lessons learned for process improvement. Table 15-1 displays a tool that might be helpful for capturing the information.

Lastly, we should celebrate every completed deliverable, no matter how small. Part of the psychology of feeling successful is promoted by appreciating accomplishment. Team members who feel they are not accomplishing anything will become less productive than those who perceive the value of what they are doing. This feeling of success ultimately makes the cost and schedule control of the project easier because the team perpetuates the efficiencies needed to accomplish the work.

Deliverable	Baseline Effort	Actual Effort	Baseline Duration	Actual Duration	Baseline Cost	Actual Cost	Issues Encountered

Table 15-1. Form for Capturing Metrics on Completed Deliverables

16 ARCHIVING COST AND SCHEDULE DATA FOR CONTINUOUS PROCESS IMPROVEMENT

Once the deliverable is complete, the cost and schedule performance metrics should be archived in a data collection information system. The use of the deliverable-oriented WBS throughout the project has set up a structure that can capture, as well as structure, the information so it can be retrieved based on specific, tangible components, parts, configuration items, or functions that may be the same as those required on other similar projects.

This repeatability allows information such as the effort it really took to complete the deliverables, the true costs and durations involved, the issues that had to be dealt with, and how well the corrective actions worked to be correlated with the same information on those same items or functions used on similar projects. These correlated data are invaluable for eliminating the guesswork and improving the initiation and planning processes used on future similar projects. Each piece of information will help estimate the effort for the next work package, balance the scope to the budget, help identify risk, help understand the work flow, etc. These little process improvements are the ones that tend to add up to major cost savings and to raise that probability of success.

And success is what it's all about.

INDEX